Leaving Yesterday Behind is a book I was privileged to read in manuscript form. It is a book, easily read, that addresses important matters. The book contains anecdotal material that enforces biblical principles and, therefore, is also practical. You may not agree with everything in it, but Bill Hines' work will stimulate your thinking and inform you. It is *eminently* useful.

Dr. Jay E. Adams, author and pastor.

The reader will find *Leaving Yesterday Behind* a refereshing source of help. Bill helps the reader focus upon those attitudes which perpetuate yesterday's problem. He demonstrates how to use the biblical tools to break free of these debilitating characteristics. The new believer and the mature Christian will be encouraged by the storyline of Jean who uses these principles to find release and peace.

Dr. Howard A. Eyrich, Author and Director of Counsel, Trinity Bible College and Seminary.

Bill Hines has done us a great service in his book *Leaving Yesterday Behind*. Bill combines sound theology with numerous examples to assure us that, through Christ, we really can break free from the problems of our past. The style is readable, the content stimulating. I enjoyed reading it and heartily recommend it.

Dr. K. Scott Oliphint, Author and Profesor of Apologetics, Westminster Theological Seminary.

Our Christian newspaper reaches approximately 100,000 readers per month, and a worldwide Internet audience. In an area abundant in so-called 'Christian' counsellors we specifically sought out Bill Hines to write a monthly biblical counselling column. Through personal interaction, the reports of other people we respect, and his writings (among them *Leaving Yesterday Behind*), Bill has proved to us that he is a rare treasure in the late twentieth-century Christian church – a compassionate, biblical counsellor with maturity, theological understanding, and the courage to stand lovingly for truth, even when others do not.

John Dywer, Editor of the *Dallas/Ft. Worth Heritage*.

LEAVING YESTERDAY BEHIND

A Victim No More

WILLIAM L. HINES

Christian Focus

Cases described in this book

All of the events described in these pages are those which do exist in the lives of actual people. Many of these examples are composites to protect confidentiality. Names and certain details of these composites are changed yet the basic thrust of the stories is true. The reader will, no doubt, find him or herself in many of these stories as we all face similar trials in life (1 Cor. 10:13).

The author can be contacted at
Covenant Ministries, Inc.
P.O. Box 121235
Fort Worth, Texas 76121-1235
(817) 738-2660

© William L. Hines
ISBN 1 85792 313 8
Published in 1997
by
Christian Focus Publications
Geanies House, Fearn, Ross-shire,
IV20 1TW, Great Britain.

Cover design by Donna Macleod

Printed by Guernsey Press

Contents

To Joy Hines
who departed this world
to be with her Lord, March 1994
and to
Robert Hines
who continues the fight without her
but never alone.

Parents who worked hard to make
all my yesterdays a foundation of
hope for the future.

Acknowledgments

I want to thank Malcolm Maclean of Christian Focus Publications for his helpful suggestions and encouragement and to the editorial staff for the willingness and enthusiasm they have shown in taking on this project.

There have been several people who offered editing and content suggestions along the way. I want to thank Deborah Collins, Mark and Karen Hines, Linda Hines, Scott and Peggy Oliphint, Thom Notaro, Jay Adams, John and Grace Dwyer and Robert Hines. Your efforts have been a great blessing to me and I trust to others as well.

Being a person who needs a lot of pushing to get things done I must recognize some key people who kept telling me to 'Write it!' Among them were: John Trent, who provided words of encouragement as well as many of the 'how to's' of writing; Howard Eyrich, who I am privileged to have as both a mentor and friend; Scott Oliphint, whose keen mind for theology and passion for its application to life had helped me stay focused on the purpose, and my wife, Kathy, who put up with many late nights and awkward schedules so that the work could be accomplished. Yours was the understanding and encouragement I greatly needed.

I would also like to recognize four churches and pastors in the Ft. Worth/Dallas area which have been of significant help in the work of Covenant Ministries and, therefore, have been of invaluable assistance to the formation of the ideas contained within these pages. Dr. Ted Kitchens and Dr. Chad

Winsor of Christ Chapel Bible Church; Rev. Tom Ferrell of Arlington Presbyterian Church (PCA); Rev. Skip Ryan and Rev. Bill Lamberth of Park Cities Presbyterian Church (PCA); and Rev. Michael Sharrett and 'my' church family at Fort Worth Presbyterian Church (PCA).

I must also include the members of the 'Board of Directors' of Covenant Ministries, Inc. Friends who care not only for the work of the ministry but who have demonstrated their concern for me and my family. Michael Sharrett, Steve Jones and Brad and Julie Beauchamp, you have my gratitude and respect.

Thanks are also due to the many people who have shared their stories and lives with me over the years. It is an honor to be a part of your pilgrimage. And to those who have supported the counseling and seminar ministry through financial gifts and prayer, may God bless you for your investment in the lives of others.

Finally, there are also five very important people who have influenced this work in a profound way and continue to remind their Daddy that God's joy and mercy is never far away. A heartfelt thankyou to Michelle, Kristin, Austin, Elise and Anna.

Introduction

Christians aren't perfect nor do they all experience a sense of peace. In fact, many are just plain miserable, feeling as if there is a great weight around their necks which prevents them from pressing on and enjoying what they understood the Christian life would be. They thought that because God is in their lives they should be free of the struggles that weigh them down or, at least, those struggles ought to be easier to overcome.

The truth is, however, that the same things that hurt the rest of the world hurt Christians too. Christians grow up in the homes of alcoholic parents or experience the trauma of incest and a number of unspeakable abuses from those who are the guardians of their well being. None of us is immune to the attitudes and behaviors that eat away at the soul. But the struggles don't have to be of such tragic proportions to have a negative effect. Perhaps it is the sense of inadequacy that comes from a father who was home but paid little attention to us or never had a kind word to say. Maybe the most bitter memories are traced to the mother who demanded perfection but did little to help her children develop character. Some homes are so full of cynicism, permissiveness, harshness or cruel manipulations that the children just don't sense that they are loved very much or worth very much.

As if all of these situations weren't enough to deal with we run to the church for help only to find a 'christianized', but ultimately empty, pop-psychology or the 'let go and let God' attitude that increases our sense of guilt but offers no real help. That is not the way God means it to be.

This book was originally conceived because I found so many people who believed they were destined to turn out like their parents. It was written because I have a deep belief, rooted in Scripture itself, that we can and must find our truest identity not in our earthly parentage but from God Himself. I believe that regardless of a person's past it is possible to make a break with the cycles of sin and disappointment that have dogged him or her, perhaps for a very long time. The perspective of this book takes humanity's dilemma seriously and will show that at the heart of humanity's most intense struggle is the heart of a merciful God, ready and willing to do for us what we are unable to do for ourselves and were never designed to do alone.

God uses processes to change people. He is aware of the sin we commit and the sin committed against us and He has a plan to deal with both. His plan matures us into the people He desires us to be and in a way that allows us to minister to the world around us – even those who have hurt us the most. In the following pages we will examine God's way of allowing us to understand the past, deal with it and leave it behind as we press on to a fulfilling life significantly freed from the pain that we have lived with for so long. Free to love Him, free to grow up to be like Him.

May all who read these pages pursue the Lord with all diligence, thus finding their load lighter and their path clear.

Bill Hines
Fort Worth, Texas 1997

Section 1

The Problem

We have met the enemy and it is us. *(POGO)*

There is not a righteous man on earth who does what is right and never sins. *(Ecclesiastes 7:20 NIV)*

A man without the Spirit of God does not do evil against his will, under pressure, as though he were taken by the scruff of the neck and dragged into it; no, he does it spontaneously and voluntarily. *(Martin Luther, 1530)[1]*

The true Christian's nostril is to be continually attentive to the inner cesspool. (*C.S. Lewis,* Letters to Malcolm: Chiefly on Prayer, *p. 98*)

The LORD looks down from heaven on the sons of men to see if there are any who understand, any who seek God. All have turned aside, they have together become corrupt; there is no one who does good, not even one. *(Psalm 14:2-3, NIV)*

Chapter 1

What is My Problem
and Who is to Blame?

Jean's Story

So many wonderful things had happened in her life that Jean felt bad about feeling so bad. The circumstances of her upbringing were very sad but she left all of that behind when she trusted in Christ as her personal Savior. Having received God's forgiveness for her sins and God's healing for the sins that had been committed against her, she knew life was going to turn out just like she had always hoped. Her new husband was a wonderful Christian man who took his responsibilities as a provider and spiritual leader very seriously. Yet in spite of all of that there seemed to be a dark cloud that hung about her. She was haunted by an ongoing depression she could not explain. Had Christianity not 'worked'? Was there something wrong with her?

Understanding Jean's past helps us understand her present situation. Jean had been born into a wealthy northwestern family. Her father was a salesman for a large pharmaceutical company and quickly climbed the success ladder. A self-professed workaholic, he was often away from home on business. When he was home he was often angry, critical, and drunk, and deferred to Jean's mother on family matters. It was later discovered that for most of Jean's life he had kept a mistress in another town.

Jean's mother was a socialite with her finger on the pulse

13

of what was 'in' and 'out' and 'proper' for herself, her children, and her husband. She was a very determined woman with little sympathy for weakness and a very defensive posture concerning her own weaknesses such as her alcoholism and manipulative control over her family. While many women would have been devastated over her husband's infidelity, she used it to strengthen her grip on him. Divorce would not have been advantageous to his career or their social standing.

Jean has many early memories which are painful and bolster her feelings of inadequacy. One such memory is that her mother refused to allow her to be ill because, to her, illness was a sign of weakness. At times this intolerance led to severe illness because her mother would wait so long to take her to the doctor.

From her earliest recollections Jean could not please her parents. Nothing was ever done well enough for them. Even her near perfect grades and achievements were met with cynicism. She so feared her parents' harsh criticism that she cried herself to sleep every night for her entire third grade school year because she feared telling them that she had lost a library book. She later discovered she had, unknowingly, returned the book on time.

Life didn't improve as Jean grew older. She resented the criticism and drunken 'lectures'. All of Jean's attempts to please or draw close to her parents ended in bitter withdrawal. The answer became clear to Jean and at the first opportunity to be rid of 'them' she married Steve. It was not long, however, before she discovered that she had married an alcoholic, work-a-holic, adulterous man just like her father. So after a difficult pregnancy, miscarriage and painful meddling by her parents, Jean found herself depressed and divorced. Jean had discovered, very painfully, that her attempts to be rid of her parents had resulted in disaster and had served only to further convince them that she needed their influence.

Emotionally drained and feeling broken Jean tried to 'lose' herself in a new career. She soon made friends with another woman in the firm who invited her to church. Jean politely refused the numerous invitations, thinking that church held very little hope or interest for her since her parents had been faithful attenders through the years. After all, she was trying desperately *not* to turn out like them.

After several months her friend once again extended an invitation. This time she was invited to attend a Christmas program. Jean accepted since she did enjoy hearing Christmas music. But this church was different. The message was about a very personal God and the people seemed genuine. They weren't perfect, but there was something about them that was interesting and full of hope. In the coming weeks she discovered that God is a personal God and that she could have a relationship with Him through faith in Jesus Christ. The promise that through the death and resurrection of Jesus she could find forgiveness for her sins and emotional healing from the sins committed against her was, to Jean, the first hope for a bright future she could remember.

Attending weekly Bible study became a mainstay in Jean's life. She felt as though her life could not get any better. David also attended the Bible study Jean had become a part of. He was bright and sensitive and caught her eye right away. More importantly he captured her heart as well.

Up to this point in her life her experience with men had been dismal. Now she had met someone who was strong enough to be sensitive and committed enough to provide leadership she could depend on. David saw in her a woman who had embraced whole-heartedly her new faith and someone who was dedicated to living the rest of her life in a way that would please the God she had come to love. After a whirlwind courtship Jean and David were married and settled in to what promised to be a most fulfilling life together. It was a wonderful relationship, but some of the old problems began to surface.

David was bewildered at first to walk in from work and find his wife deeply depressed. He lovingly searched for answers from her but found she had none. He had known of her bouts with depression but had not experienced them firsthand. Jean also experienced physiological illness with no concrete diagnosis. Her mother continued to intrude as often as she could, even seeking to undermine Jean's relationship with her new in-laws by openly gossiping to them about Jean and David. Rarely did she have any contact with her parents that did not leave her hurt and depressed.

Jean knew that if she did not find some help she would be in danger of destroying herself, her marriage, and robbing the joy from her new relationship with the God she had grown to love very deeply. Desperate for answers, Jean sought biblical counseling. In our first session she shared her story with me. With a background like hers what hope could I give her? She wanted to know whether she was destined to turn out like her parents. Was she? Are you and I destined to turn out like our parents?

Many today have grown into adulthood reaping what they

have come to consider an evil harvest in life. Like Jean, they live with pain they did not cause. That pain takes many forms but it can often be traced to such things as parental alcoholism, sexual or verbal abuse, neglect, perfectionism, negativism or a number of other negative conditions while growing up. It doesn't seem fair that people should suffer because the guardians of their well-being have hurt them. But if you are like many people you have experienced that unfairness. Someone has hurt you deeply. Will you, in turn, hurt someone else?

How did the problem begin?

Are the sins of the fathers really visited upon the children (Exod. 20:5-6)? That question is troublesome to contemplate, but it brings up an important truth in Scripture; the truth that often people are blessed or cursed because of the righteousness or sin of one person or a group of persons. The greatest example of corporate cursing is Adam, our first human father. Adam sinned, and as a result, every human being who has ever lived has been born with a fallen, or sinful, nature. You and I did not eat of the forbidden fruit in the Garden of Eden, but the representative head of the human race, Adam, did. With Adam as our representative we share the consequences of his sin (Rom. 5:12-21).

> ...just as sin entered the world through one man, and death through sin, and in this way death came to all men... (Rom. 5:12)

In the same way, you and I have not lived a perfect life, died on the cross and risen again. Yet the blessing of the work of Christ is applied to all who believe.

For if, by the trespass of the one man, death reigned
through that one man, how much more will those who
receive God's abundant provision of grace and of the
gift of righteousness reign in life through the one man,
Jesus Christ (Rom. 5:17).

So we see that the sin of one man, Adam, brought death on
all who were born from him. We see also that through the
righteous act of one man, Jesus, life was given to all who
were born not according to the flesh but according to the
Spirit after Him.

In like manner God also works through families. We have
seen how we were affected by Adam and Eve. But consider
too the family of Noah (saving his family based on the favor
Noah had found with God), and the family of Abraham
(establishing the chosen people, the Jewish race, through
the faith of Abraham). Peter declared at Pentecost that 'the
promise is for you and your children and for all who are far
off – for all whom the Lord our God will call' (Acts 2:39).

Perhaps it isn't so difficult to understand the sins of the
fathers being passed on to other generations after all. The
sinful nature is passed on biologically as we are born into
bodies which will deteriorate and die; spiritually, the sin
nature is passed on in our predisposition to sin; and
behaviorally, the sin nature is evidenced as we learn to model
the behavior of our parents as we grow up. Learning language
and mannerisms are only the tip of the modeling iceberg.
We also learn such things as ways of dealing with stress,
anger, speaking to strangers, the respect for parents and
others and where we place value. In short, how we live and
what we live for are learned, primarily, from our parents.

Are we to conclude from all of this that we are born blessed or cursed, and that settles the matter? No! We must look at the other side of the same coin – individual responsibility.

Individual responsibility

Did all of the Israelites who were delivered from slavery in Egypt through Moses get to the land of promise? No. Most died in unbelief before receiving the promise because although they heard the Word of God and saw the miracles, they did not personally appropriate it by faith. While corporate blessing and cursing is little understood in our day, it might well be said that the individual is overemphasised. Yet we find both supported in the same verse. Look at Exodus 20:5-6:

' ...for I the LORD your God, am a jealous God, punishing the children for the sins of the fathers to the third and fourth generation of those who hate me, but showing love to a thousand generations of those who love me and keep my commandments.'

Who, in these verses, is responsible for the blessing and cursing of the generations? The individuals who sin or love God. Just as Adam was personally responsible for what he did to himself and his descendents, so are we. All through Scripture we see the call for individuals to repent and respond to God by personal faith. Psalm 103:17 tells us that God's love is with all who keep His covenant and remember to obey His precepts. The prophet Ezekiel makes this very clear in chapter 18. Here is an illustration of a father who is righteous, but he has a son who is wicked. If the wicked son dies, is he saved by his father's righteousness? No, he dies a sinner. The illustration goes on to ask if that wicked man has a son who sees his father's wickedness and chooses to be righteous, will he be condemned because of his father's wickedness? Again, the answer is no. He will live because of his choice for righteousness. The argument is summarized in Ezekiel 18:20:

> The soul who sins is the one who will die. The son will not share the guilt of the father, nor will the father share the guilt of the son. The righteousness of the righteous man will be credited to him, and the wickedness of the wicked will be charged against him.

Jesus Himself calls for people to come to Him personally (Matt. 28:11). His apostle, Paul, calls for personal faith in Jesus to be exercised:

> ...if you confess with your mouth, 'Jesus is Lord,' and believe in your heart that God raised Him from the dead, you will be saved

and

> ...everyone who calls on the name of the Lord shall be saved.

While God makes provision for benefits and blessings to the child of godly parents, it does not guarantee them.[2] It is the children who exhibit faith by personally obeying God who are heirs to the promises.

Two sides of the same coin

How do we balance the teaching of Scripture on the corporate and individual blessing and cursing of people? We see it as two sides of the same coin, which must be held in balance. To neglect the corporate nature of blessing and cursing may lead to isolationism and irresponsibility where culture and future generations are concerned. To neglect the individual aspect of blessing and cursing may lead us to false assumptions about the destiny of our children and our personal responsibility to make godly decisions. We must have a balanced perspective.

Our own personal histories

So what is the problem? Is it our parents? Our environment? Not primarily. Our problem goes all the way back to our first parents, Adam and Eve. Since their sin we have all been born in a state of sin and continue, this side of heaven, to struggle with sin's effects (more about those effects in Section 3). Regardless of what our modern culture says, we don't disobey God because we suffer low self-esteem. We disobey because we are sinners. The environment we were born into may give direction to our sin but we must make no mistake about it – we were going to sin in some way because we were born alienated from and rebellious towards God.

If we are going to *leave yesterday behind* we must do some personal evaluation of our past. But we do this not in order to shift blame on someone else. Rather, we want to recognize trends and influences that have moulded our lives so that we can, from this point on, begin to take responsibility for our lives and, with the help of God, change those behaviors and attitudes that need to be changed.

Section 2

The Promise

But he was pierced for our transgressions, he was crushed for our iniquities; the punishment that brought us peace was upon him, and by his wounds we are healed. *(Isaiah 53:5)*

Now there was a man in Jerusalem called Simeon, who was righteous and devout. He was waiting for the consolation of Israel, and the Holy Spirit was upon him. It had been revealed to him by the Holy Spirit that he would not die before he had seen the Lord's Christ.

Moved by the Spirit, he went into the temple courts. When the parents brought in the child Jesus to do for him what the custom of the Law required, Simeon took him in his arms and praised God, saying:

'Sovereign Lord, as you have promised, you now dismiss your servant in peace. For my eyes have seen your salvation, which you have prepared in the sight of all people, a light for revelation to the Gentiles and for glory to your people Israel.' *(Luke 2:25-32)*

Chapter 2

The Promise of Life

Jean discovered very painfully that her parents were not her deepest problem. She found that regardless of who our parents are we all share the legacy of the sin nature left us by Adam and Eve.

But while Jean had understood a little bit about the sin nature she had failed to grasp how the depth and horror of her own sin had hindered her own spiritual growth. Up to this point each time she faced problems she would immediately think about how her parents had in some way caused or influenced them. By understanding the curse she was under as a descendent of Adam she discovered that the real issues she faced in life all related to her fallen nature.

In many ways that was a relief. While she had resented her parents for the way they had hurt her she also felt sorry for them. As their daughter she had experienced both resentment and compassion for her parents. Now she understood why. They were under the same curse she was. While they were responsible for what they had done to her Jean understood that she too had hurt people and justified her actions.

Beyond that, however, Jean learned through her study of the sin of Adam and Eve that sin not only destroyed paradise for mankind but it deeply hurt the heart of God the Creator. It was with this understanding that Jean's own heart began to break. She had spent most of her life being angry with what her parents had done to her without a thought concerning what she had done to God. She had often struggled with how she could love her parents and how she could love herself, but now as she stared reality in the face her question became, 'How could such a loving and holy God possibly love me?' She felt so evil and ashamed she wondered if she could ever face God again. It was then that a valued friend directed her attention to the scarlet thread that runs throughout Scripture from the first animal sacrifice to the cross of the Savior. Burdened with the weight of her sinfulness, Jean focused on the garden, the cross, and the promise of a merciful God.

The stage is set

Adam and Eve had sinned and been found out. They were ashamed, afraid and blaming one another and even God for what had happened. What was their excuse? Did they lack information? No. God had told them they would die if they ate of the fruit of that particular tree. Although they clearly understood there would be death, I'm sure that they had no idea what a long, agonizing and multi-faceted death it would be. They soon found out it wasn't, at first, a cessation of bodily functions, that would come later. No, this death involved every relationship they had or ever would have. It also involved every relationship you and I would have. Theirs was indeed a curse with far-reaching implications that settled as a dark cloud upon all of life. But in the midst of this curse came a promise.

> So the LORD God said to the serpent, 'Because you have done this, cursed are you above all the livestock and all the wild animals! You will crawl on your belly and you will eat dust all the days of your life. And I will put enmity between you and the woman, and between your offspring and hers; he will crush your head, and you will strike his heel' (Gen. 3:14-15).

In this portion of Scripture we have the first mention of the ministry of Christ. Christ is 'the seed of the woman' and the One who 'will crush your [the serpent's] head'. This establishes the battle of the ages between God's people (those who follow Christ) and Satan's people (those who do not follow Christ). Note also the outcome of the battle alluded to here. Satan's blow is to the heel. Certainly an agonizing injury but not fatal. Christ's blow, however, *is* fatal – crushing Satan's head. We get a further glimpse of God's provision in Genesis 3:21:

> The LORD God made garments of skin for Adam and his wife and clothed them.

How had Adam and Eve tried to cover their shame once they knew they were naked? With leaves. God, however, in dramatic fashion gave them a glimpse of what was to come by shedding the innocent blood of animals to cover the sin of the man and woman. It is important to note that God performed this act on behalf of man, man did not do it for himself. Man's attempts were futile at best. From this point on we see a trail of blood throughout the Old Testament, from Abel's sacrifice through the system of animal sacrifices, leading to the cross of Christ, which was the ultimate fulfilment. After the death of Jesus no further blood sacrifice would ever be needed.

How we cover up

I have been told by victims of incest that one of the most difficult aspects of such abuse is the shame they feel even years later. Even though they know intellectually that the abuse was not their fault they still are burdened with guilt and shame. Whether we experience shame as a victim or shame from our own wrong choices we must learn the lesson that Adam and Eve learned. We must realize that all our own feeble attempts to cover our shame fall far short of what is necessary. As God covered the shame of Adam and Eve with the skins of innocent animals so He covers us with the shed blood of Christ. Our own attempts to deal with shame apart from His provision will always fall short. In many ways our own behavior is simply a way to 'cover up' the shame we feel. Our 'fig leaves' might be alcoholism, materialism, promiscuity, gossip, perfectionism or a host of other behaviors and attitudes we think will make us feel better about who we are. But they will always fall short. There is only one answer for our guilt and shame.[3]

How we begin to live

The promise in the midst of the curse was for One who would redeem man from the effects of the curse. The promise was that One would come and free us from the entanglements of our broken relationship with God, self, others and nature.[4] That is exactly what the life, death and resurrection of Jesus did. It broke the stranglehold of sinfulness! Just as sin and death reigned for those born in Adam, now righteousness and life reign for those born again in Christ. It is not as though the penalty for sin goes unpaid. It is just that it is paid by Christ Himself on our behalf. The apostle Paul says that when Jesus died He identified with us in such an intimate way that we died with Him. That is the argument of Romans 6. Our identity with Jesus is such that when He died, we died, and when He rose, we rose.

> If we have been united with him like this in his death, we will certainly also be united with him in his resurrection. For we know that our old self was crucified with him so that the body of sin might be done away with, that we should no longer be slaves to sin – because anyone who has died has been freed from sin (Rom. 6:5-7).

If we keep in mind that the penalty for sin is death, these verses are incredibly liberating. If Jesus died and satisfied this death requirement and we died with Him, we truly are free of sin's reign in our lives. Further Paul says that just as surely as we died with Him, we rose with Him. We rose to a new life free of the entanglements of sin. For the first time ever we have the capacity to please God. We are no longer under the dominion of sin, but righteousness. We have a new Master.

Why do we still sin?

You may be asking at this point, 'If all of this is true, why do Christians still sin?' To answer the question we must remind ourselves of the unfolding, progressive nature of the kingdom of God.

The kingdom now and then

I was told once by a man who had studied the Second World War in depth, that once the Allies landed on the continent of Europe the war was over. I looked at him a little puzzled, so he continued by saying there was no question that the firepower, manpower and military intelligence of the Allies would eventually conquer Hitler and his armies. It was just a matter of going through the process of completing what was bound to happen.

When Jesus was on earth He spoke of the kingdom of God as being near (Matt. 4:17), as yet to come (Matt. 6:10) and as having already come (Matt. 12:28). How are you and I to understand the progressive nature of this kingdom? God's plan for man has, from the beginning, been of an unfolding nature. Who knew, besides God, that when He first promised the Messiah in Genesis 3 the road to Calvary would take so many turns and involve the death of God the Son? Yet, as more and more of God's plan began to be revealed, man caught glimpses of the suffering servant that not only would die for His people, but would also reign over them and make all things right.

In the same way, Jesus and His apostles spoke of the progressive nature of His kingdom. His would not be a kingdom that happened all at once, but it would unfold in the hearts of His people now and would be fully realized in the new heaven and the new earth one day in the future.

Does it seem to you that I have strayed from the question of why we still sin? I really haven't, because by understanding the nature of the emerging kingdom, we begin to understand the battle of our hearts. The kingdom has come to us who have trusted in Christ. The King now reigns in our hearts, but the final liberation of our hearts is yet to come. We look with eager anticipation to that day when we are finally set free and we rejoice now in the fact that victory is at hand, all the while remembering that we are part of the process of liberation. For it is our duty to surrender the strongholds of resistance in our hearts to Christ to bring them under His dominion.

My father had the privilege of being one of the thousands of American soldiers who participated in the liberation of Europe in the Second World War. He recalls the scene as they marched into a newly liberated section of Germany. The road was lined with men who had been set free from a slave-labour camp. They were in their striped prison uniforms and in pitiful condition. They were sick, emaciated, some without teeth. He recalls one man in particular crouched at the side of the road trying to eat a sugarbeet. In his pitiful condition he flashed a toothless grin, waving at the troops, appearing to glory in his new freedom. Did this man have significant challenges in the future? Certainly. Was it going to be easy to put the horrors of the labour camps behind him and get the medical help he needed? Not at all. But for the first time, perhaps in many years, he had hope and he was free to pursue life.

If you are a Christian, the Holy Spirit has liberated your heart from slavery to sin. The reign of sin has been broken and you are free to serve your true King. It won't be easy, but it will happen as you fight the battles He leads you in and surrender to Him the areas of resistance. The victory is assured. The only question is, how much of that victory do you want to experience in this life? What would you have said to the man from the labour camp if, upon his release, he had chosen to stay in the camp, eating the same poor food, doing the same demeaning work? I hope you would have tried to encourage him that outside of the camp there was help and hope and that no matter how great the struggle to regain his life, it would be worth it. What will you say to yourself? Do you want the kind of life Jesus died for? If so, read on. You need to know God's plan for the liberation of your heart. You need to understand God's process for *leaving yesterday behind*.

Section 3

The Process

The choicest believers, who are assuredly freed from the condemning power of sin, ought yet to make it their business all their days to mortify the indwelling power of sin.[5] *(John Owen)*

My soul clings to Thee; Thy right hand upholds me. *(Psalm 63:8, NASB)*

In the same way, count yourselves dead to sin but alive to God in Christ Jesus. Therefore do not let sin reign in your mortal body so that you obey its evil desires.

Do not offer the parts of your body to sin, as instruments of wickedness, but rather offer yourselves to God, as those who have been brought from death to life; and offer the parts of your body to him as instruments of righteousness. For sin shall not be your master, because you are not under law, but under grace. *(Romans 6:11-14)*

Chapter 3

Grace for the Journey

The concept of the promise of God was exciting, but the realization that the promise of total forgiveness was true in her life was life-changing to Jean. She felt as though she were walking on clouds for the first few days. Then her mother phoned and in typical fashion 'cut Jean down to size' for not phoning her more often. Jean hung up the phone in tears but instead of calling her husband in a panic this time she sat down and talked to herself for a few minutes. 'Thirty minutes ago I was delighted with life and hopeful. Now I'm not sure it's all worth it. Why do I allow my mother to affect me this way?' Then Jean remembered about the progressive nature of the kingdom of God and how she had to relinquish the strongholds of her heart to Him as she discovered those areas of resistance. God didn't expect her to be rid of all the hurt and heal the scars immediately. It was a process. But how was she to engage the process? Instead of continuing to beat herself up over the same old things, Jean set out to discover how she could implement the truths of Scripture and move on in her relationship with God.

I can remember as a young Christian listening to Billy Graham on television and feeling guilty that I could not communicate as well as he. Never mind that I was only 15 and had been a Christian less than a year. I thought that was how a Christian, any Christian, was supposed to articulate biblical principles. I have known other people who have experienced the same kinds of pressure. We judge our own spirituality by looking at others. Then we feel guilty and become discouraged, which hinders our growth even further. I was a well-meaning 15-year-old who wanted to follow Christ. Was it really too much to ask to be on Billy Graham's level? Yes, it was. There was a big part of salvation I did not understand. When I finally began to see that salvation is a word which applies, not only to becoming a Christian, but also to growing as a Christian, I began to see life as an amazing journey. A journey which leads through many trials and joys, as I am conformed more and more into the person God desires me to be. Like Jean I had to find strength for the journey. I found, somewhat to my surprise, that the key to the strength I needed was a better understanding of the grace of God.

Going with the flow

It didn't happen very often, but that day it did. The dam at the nearby reservoir was opened, filling the various tributaries below with more water than usual. My friend Ernest and I rushed down to the river to take advantage of all the free water on a hot afternoon.

There was a small fork in the river and at first we were content to enjoy the calm, cool waters of this side pool. It wasn't long, however, before we began to wonder what it would be like to be out in the middle of the large river, out where the water was moving quite rapidly. I must confess I knew better than to go out there. I had been fishing in the mountains of New Mexico and had experienced the force of the river as the rushing water swept me off my feet. I had even heard my Grandfather tell about the time he waded out too far and was swept helplessly downstream waiting for the river to deliver him to the shallow side waters unharmed. With all that valuable life experience behind me, Ernest and I jumped into the rushing waters.

The first few seconds were exhilarating. I couldn't believe how fast we were being swept along. It didn't look nearly so swift from the side. Then panic set in. How were we going to get back to the side? I must have had the same look of terror on my face that I saw on Ernest's. I remember the realization that I was completely at the mercy of the flow of the river. Wherever it wanted to take me I was bound to go. I had very little say in what happened to me. The only thing I could do was to co-operate with the river, keep my head up and away from rocks and wait until I was given the opportunity to grab the side. We were given that opportunity, and climbed out a considerable distance from where we'd begun. Though unspoken at the time, I'm sure Ernest shared my sense of being spared. Strangely enough, when we told the story at school the next day there was no talk of fear — only triumph.

The river illustrates a great truth. The truth that there is a flow to life. Like the river, history is going somewhere by God's design. We may be willing to watch from the side, as others are swept along. We may even cheer them on as they experience the exhilaration of life, but each of us must ask ourselves some questions: 'Am I willing to step out and experience the sweeping changes that God says He can make in my life? Am I willing to trust the One who controls the flow of life? Will I allow Him to take and change those patterns of thinking and behavior that hold me back, or do I prefer to hold on to them as a security blanket that I never quite outgrow?'

A changed attitude towards change

The only acceptable answer for the Christian to those questions is, 'Yes, I choose to allow God to change me.' To change is painful, but perhaps not as painful as we fear. That is because God provides us with a great truth that, properly applied, changes our attitude about change. That truth is that His grace is sufficient to give us all we need for the greatest journey of all – the journey from sin and death through this life and into the eternal kingdom (2 Cor. 12:9). Remember too, that while it was foolish for my friend and I to jump into that river, it is never foolish to allow the flow of God's grace to take us wherever He wills.

An old word with new meaning

When I think of getting into the flow of what God is doing, I think of grace as the water which moves me along. Grace is there at the beginning of the Christian life, it is there at the end and it is at every point in between. There is never a time in the Christian's life when grace is not operating. As the water in the river, it completely envelopes us and moves us along. But what is it? I have found that the older I get, the broader the application of this great teaching of Scripture.

In our culture grace is often thought of as a personal virtue, but the New Testament sense of grace is that of unmerited favor.[6]

The classic verse on salvation by grace shows this quite forcefully:

For it is by grace you have been saved, through faith – and this not from yourselves, it is the gift of God – not by works, so that no one can boast. For we are God's

workmanship, created in Christ Jesus to do good works,
which God prepared in advance for us to do (Eph. 2:8-10).

We are not to boast of our salvation because there was
absolutely nothing we did to deserve it. *God had mercy on
us*. Note also that all the good works we will ever perform
are also by grace. For without the grace of God we would
never have been brought into a relationship of faith, and
therefore, we would never have been able to please God at
all (Heb. 11:6). Further evidence of this present tense of
God's grace towards us is in 2 Corinthians 6:1-2 where Paul
tells us that God's grace, God's favor, is now. Romans 5:2
describes it as standing in grace.

It is because of this present ministry of grace in our lives
that we see grace as divine enablement. It is God's grace
which enables us to live the Christian life. That is why Paul
begins many of his letters by saying 'grace to you...'. It is
by grace we have been saved, are being saved and will be
saved.

The nature of grace

Someone reading this will no doubt say, 'If God's grace is
so available, I'll just do whatever I want because I know I'll
be forgiven.' The person who says such a thing, however,
doesn't understand the nature of grace. By grace we are given
a new motivation in life. To live as a non-Christian (living
in sin) is continuing in captivity. Captivity is the opposite
of what grace was designed to provide. Grace sets us free.
The New Testament defines freedom not as licence to
participate in sin without consequence, but rather as the
opportunity to choose obedience to God (see Gal. 5:1; Heb.
11:6; 1 Peter 2:16).

If we are free we must live as free people. This means refusing to accept the self talk which continues to condemn (for there is no condemnation for those who are in Christ – Rom. 8:1). In its place we gratefully accept His mercy which forgives and reminds us that we are His and He will empower us to serve Him faithfully. To understand grace is to understand God's forgiveness.

> For he has rescued us from the dominion of darkness and brought us into the kingdom of the Son he loves, in whom we have redemption, the forgiveness of sins (Col. 1:13,14).

Applying grace

In order to live empowered by grace we must learn how to live in grace. To do this successfully we must learn to apply His mercy, His way, as His obedient children.

His mercy

At the heart of grace is God's mercy, God's forgiveness of sinners.

It may seem strange to speak in terms of accepting His mercy, but this is a very real problem. There are many reasons why people just don't accept, with any degree of conviction, the mercy He offers them now. It is one thing to accept a future forgiveness. That seems far off and romantic. It is, however, a very different thing to live as though we are forgiven right now. Why?

1. Some don't accept God's present mercy because of a lack of understanding. They just need better teaching on what the Bible has to say about it.[7]

2. Another reason some reject God's mercy is a deep conviction that they are unforgivable. I have seen this attitude particularly in people who have been abused as children, because they were taught to think that the abuse was somehow their fault. Others may be equally plagued by a conviction that what they have done or what has been done to them is beyond God's mercy.

3. Finally, there are those who just don't want to experience God's mercy. This category may represent more of us than we care to admit. Before you say, 'That's not me!' think about it. God has always stood ready to throw aside His anger towards sin and forgive (Jer. 3:12-13). It is our resistance to confessing and turning from our sin that is the problem. Instead we create reasons why we cannot change. Some of our reasons are very convincing but in our heart of hearts we know that they are just diversions we use to try to convince ourselves that we are stuck. Because the real truth is that if we saw ourselves as really forgiven, if we admitted to ourselves that we stand in grace right now, we would be without excuse. We would have to change, and some of us love the security of the sin we have always known to give it up – even for God.

After counseling a woman for a long time I became frustrated with her lack of progress. She was someone I'd had high hopes for. She was bright and sensitive with great questions and what seemed to be a hopeful countenance. However, as the counseling sessions went on week after week she always had some reason why my suggestions couldn't work for her. She was pleasant, but unwavering in her contentions that she just couldn't change. Finally, I suggested to her that perhaps she didn't want to change. Her retort was sharp and piercing, 'Do you think I want to live like this? Do you think I enjoy the pain I've been through?' I told her what I thought was that she had become so accustomed to her problems, they had become her security blanket. The fear of life without all the problems was far more frightening than continuing in them. That's the deception of sin. We speak of it as our greatest enemy, yet we hold it close, refusing to let go. Any change is difficult, but we must entrust ourselves to the God of mercy who cares for His people.

His way

Besides accepting God's mercy, we must accept His methods. It is amazing to me how so many people think God is there to do their bidding. It is like the defeated General who said, 'I surrender, and here are my demands.' When we come to God to receive His forgiveness, we surrender to Him. We don't tell Him how to forgive and change us, He tells us. After all, God created life and He knows how it works. We must live the way God intended and when change is necessary, we must be willing to give up what He wants us to give up and become what He wants us to become. As Jesus said in Luke 9:23-24:

> 'If anyone would come after me, he must deny himself and take up his cross daily and follow me. For whoever wants to save his life will lose it, but whoever will lose his life for me will save it.'

As His obedient children

This brings us to the last point in applying the grace of God. We must focus on who we have become in Christ and persevere to be who we are as His children. God's children are to act like their heavenly Father. There will be more about this family relationship in Chapter 4. For our present discussion it is important to understand that in our efforts to become more like Christ grace is at work as we work. Think of it as a muscle. The muscle tones and strengthens as it is used. Let the muscle just lie there and it will wither and weaken. Grace is applied as we use it. An important step in the application of grace is to get out there and work at living the Christian life by obeying His commands. When we obey God in our attitudes and actions, grace grows stronger in us and we are able to reflect the image of God in increasing measure. Christians work hard at life simply because we love God. We no longer work out of fear of His judgment, but out of devotion to Him because we belong to Him.

The ever-flowing waterfall of grace

I am amazed by waterfalls. I enjoy the beauty and the spray, but most of all I am amazed that a great waterfall like Niagara Falls never runs out of water. Perhaps that is a simple thing, but it amazes me. Think of how many years Niagara Falls has been flowing. The more I study the grace of God the more I am amazed that, like the waterfall, His grace never runs out. But let's take the illustration even further.

Have you ever stood in a waterfall? It is quite refreshing. Think of the water as God's grace. It never runs out. Now picture yourself standing in the pool at the bottom of the falls. Water is all around you and it is flowing on your head

and down your body. You are saturated by the water. When
we think of the water as the grace of God, we are standing
in it and it is always flowing and enveloping us. The problem
is that we pull out an umbrella and divert the flow of grace.
It's all around us, it's available but it's not saturating and
refreshing us. You might be thinking how silly it would be
to stop the flow of grace in our lives, yet that is exactly what
we do when we disobey God. When we disobey, we quench
the Holy Spirit and cease to have the power that His grace
gives us to grow and please God. The sin could be many
things. It could be adultery, gossip, legalism, self-reliance,
pride or simply not thinking as a Christian – buying into the
thinking patterns of the world around us. When we are not
operating in grace, we are operating in what the Bible calls
the flesh. If we divert the flow of grace in our lives through
disobedience, we do so to our own peril.

Which comes first

The question may be asked, 'Which comes first, the
empowerment to be obedient or the act of obedience itself?'
The answer is that it always begins with the commitment to
obey, but as we obey our motivation is strengthened to obey
all the more.

A man illustrated this once for me. He told me that his
relationship with his wife had become almost unbearable
and that he thought seriously about divorce. He just could
not conjure up the feelings that he thought were necessary
to love her as God commanded. But as he began to understand that he was to love her regardless of how he felt about
her, he committed to love her in a way that would please
God. He began doing special things for her such as those

household chores she had nagged him to do for years. He began to include her in plans for the family and to seek out her suggestions for family outings. He began to take the spiritual leadership of the family which he had neglected. The result was that as he behaved in loving ways towards her his heart began to change and he developed strong feelings of love for her. Was he motivated internally or externally? The answer is both, because as he built upon the basic commitment to love her by acting in ways that a loving person would act, he found that his behavior supported and encouraged his desire for her, which further encouraged positive behavior.

How grace leaves yesterday behind

To live in grace is to live in the knowledge that God's forgiveness is real and complete. It is stepping out in faith and applying His methods and working to reflect the character of Christ faithfully. Remember an earlier illustration: the prisoner is pronounced free, but he doesn't experience that freedom until he steps out of the prison and exercises the privileges that are rightfully his. By grace, forgiveness is granted and what is left for us to do is to live in the reality that God looks on us with His favor and in doing so He empowers us to live as He desires us to.

Living in the grace of God does not mean we live in such a way as to no longer need His forgiveness. Otherwise Paul's saying, '...grace to you' (Rom. 1:7), could be taken to be encouragement to sin more so you can experience more grace. He argues just the opposite, however, in Romans 6. Living in the grace of God means being able to live in obedience to Him in increasing measure. When we think of grace we should think of it as the agent of both forgiveness and empowerment.

Grace breaks the stranglehold of sin by putting us in a new relationship with God. Before we had Christ we were dead in sin and under God's judgment. In Christ we are recipients of life and blessing (Eph. 2:1-5). We have been made His children, received a new heart and mind and we have been given His Spirit to live inside us and minister to us (Ezek. 36:25-27; 2 Cor. 5:17; Eph. 1:3-14). The 'how to' of *leaving yesterday behind* in grace is to be who we are in Christ.

As one who had always thought she had to satisfy her husband and her parents or be a failure, Jean was in awe of God's grace. His grace told her that she was fully acceptable to Him now. She learned that God would help her grow as she stepped out in obedience to Him. Her parents' demands told her she never would be acceptable, but God said she already was. She was ready now to live a life empowered by grace and to learn more about her new family in Christ.

Who are you in Christ? If you belong to Christ you are a child with a privileged position and a new identity in the family of God.

Chapter 4

A New Identity

What's the common denominator among the following: self esteem, urban gangs, school clubs, church denominations, rock star 'T' shirts, leather jackets and cult worship? The answer? They all have something to do with identity. Human beings want to be identified with something or someone. From the time we are very young we think in terms of our names, our parents and our schools as those things which help to identify, define and classify us. Humans do see identity as important, so important that we will even resort to negative, sometimes criminal behavior to 'be somebody'.

For the last fifteen years a person would be hard pressed to go through a week without hearing something about self-esteem. From infants' classrooms to high level corporate meetings self-esteem is a hot topic. Lacking self-esteem, we are told, can lead to alcoholism, child abuse, crime, poor relationships and unhappiness. Possessing self-esteem most certainly, in the minds of some, leads to fortune, self-actualization, non-possessive relationships and a general sense of personal well-being. The problem is that, despite the emphasis on self-esteem, it just hasn't worked out quite so neatly.

The reign of self-esteem
I was intrigued by an article in Newsweek Magazine with the cover title of *The Curse of Self-Esteem: What's Wrong*

With the Feel-Good Movement. This secular magazine
declared that our culture's preoccupation with self-esteem
has led us down a path of selfishness and shallowness. They
make the point that believing you are terrific isn't the same
as actually being terrific.[8] It took *Newsweek* to say what
Christians should have said all along. The preoccupation
with self has had incredible influence on the way our culture
deals with problems. It has also had considerable influence
on the way Christians have dealt with problems. Many
pulpits in evangelical circles are strangely silent on topics
such as sin. Many think that sin is just too negative a concept
and that we should talk instead of people just not reaching
their potential. The problem is that the Bible never speaks
in such terms. God says that He hates sin and sin must be
dealt with. In fact, He hates sin so much that He sent His
Son to die so that we could overcome sin's effects on our
lives. So the woman who told me that she 'cheated' on her
husband because she lacked self-esteem was wrong. She
committed adultery because she is a sinner. The answer to
her sin is not to like herself more, it is to confess her sin and
repent. That is the perspective we need. The issues of identity
have become very clouded. We need to clear the air by
answering a few important questions.

Is identity important?

Identity is extremely important. Who we are is central to
our mission in life. The problem is that the approach to
identity put forth in the pop-psychology of the last decade
is wrong. Identity in its essence does not come from within
the person. Man's identity was given to him by His Creator.
Adam was formed by God and then told what he was to do

with his life by God. Adam wasn't left in the garden of Eden and told to 'look deep within and find himself '. God communicated with Adam. He told Adam that he was made for a purpose, and that purpose was determined by God Himself.

So who are we?

At the very foundation of who we are is the image of God. Genesis 1:27 tells us:

> So God created man in his own image, in the image of God he created him; male and female he created them.

The image of God in man is central to our identity. The expression *the image of God* means simply 'made like God'. This does not mean that man is like God in every way. For instance, man is not all-knowing or infinite. But it does mean man is like God in some very important ways. Man can think, feel and make choices like God does. He is the only member of the physical created order that has a personal relationship with God. It was only man who could listen to God (Gen. 1:28) and speak to God (Gen. 3:10).[9] The animals could not.

Essentially, man is like God in that he is a person with personal attributes. Dick Keyes has said, 'Man bears the image of God in two ways. Adam was like God in the way he was and also in what he did, in his being and also in his doing.'[10] In a sense we imitate God in who we are and what we do. Keyes goes on to say that, 'A fundamental foundation stone of the Christian faith is that as man reflects God's character, he thereby realizes his own true character, identity, and selfhood. Man is not a manufactured identity, but an identity derived from his Maker.'[11]

Mirror, mirror on the wall

The concept of reflecting God's character is a helpful one. A pastor friend of mine, David Brack, had an intriguing message he used to give to high-school students. In this message he would hold up a mirror and ask them what they saw. Common responses were, 'me', 'myself' and 'the most beautiful girl in the world'. When pressed as to what they really saw they would come to the conclusion that what they saw was not themselves, but a reflection of themselves. David would go on to say that man was created, not to be God, but to reflect the image of God. All of us, like mirrors, should reflect who God is in who we are and what we do. Then David would do something that no-one expected, he threw the mirror down on the ground with a crash, breaking it into little pieces. When he picked up the mirror, which now looked like a broken car windshield, still in the frame but cracked in little pieces, he would say, 'Now what do you see?' Now the answers were more like, 'It's still a reflection of me, but it doesn't look the same. It's fragmented and distorted.'

Do you get the connection? We, like the mirror, were made to reflect the character of God, but when man sinned that image became broken and distorted. The image is still there, but no longer accurately reflects the Creator. Growing up in Christ means filling in the cracks by conforming more and more to the image of Christ, and thus more accurately reflecting the image we were designed for.

Possessing the image of God is the essence of who we

are, but there are other aspects of life that further define us. For instance, it could be said of Adam that he was man, created in the image of God and that as one possessing the Creator's image, he expressed his selfhood in performing certain tasks. Note that what he *does* is not who he is, but rather it is an extension or expression of who he is. This is important because so many of us define our personhood by where we work or what we do. Our work is important to God, but it is not who we are. Jesus, as the Son of God through whom the world was created, washed the feet of the disciples. Did that make Him less important than one of the kings of His day who would not have stooped to such a lowly task? Certainly not. It was because Jesus understood who He was that He was not threatened by being a servant. Nor should we be.

Let me say it again. What we do is important and activities such as our jobs, hobbies and avocations help define our personal callings and express our personhood. But essentially we are image bearers of our Creator. Perhaps I can help to explain this further with the help of the apostle John.

Not, 'Who are you?' but, 'Whose are you?'

When I was young there seemed to be two questions that even a little child could anticipate from a stranger. 'What's your name?' and 'Who are your parents?' and sometimes, 'What does your Dad do?' Regretably, many adults place value on children according to what their parents do for a living or what part of town they live in. That carries over to the children themselves and early on we learn which side of the tracks we are from and what that means socially.

Although some of the ramifications are regretable, we do get a sense of who we are by who our parents are. That is a big problem for many people, especially if they don't think very highly of their parents. Whether we like it or not, however, we all think of ourselves in relation to our families of origin.

Why do I make such a point of this? Simply because it is on the basis of our parentage that we can best deal with our problem past. There is a twist to this, however. The twist is that for the Christian there is a whole new way of looking at parentage. Remember in Chapter One I said that our first parents, Adam and Eve, passed on a legacy of sin to our parents who passed it on to us. That is why we have problems. There is sin in our hearts and sin in the world. The apostle John explains to us, however, that Christians have a new Father and a new family.

> Jesus answered, 'I tell you the truth, no one can enter the kingdom of God unless he is born of water and the Spirit. Flesh gives birth to flesh, but the Spirit gives birth to spirit. You should not be surprised at my saying, "You must be born again" ' (John 3:5-7).

> How great is the love the Father has lavished on us, that we should be called children of God! And that is what we are! (1 John 3:1).

There is a new birth required for entrance into the kingdom of God. To be born you must have parents. In the case of spiritual birth your Father is God himself. This means that just as your earthly parents left you a legacy of sinfulness, as a born-again Christian our heavenly Father gives you a legacy of righteousness. God gives you a whole new nature. This means that the Christian has a new family, the family of God.

Whose child are you? If you are a Christian you are God's child! When you think of yourself you should primarily think of yourself as a child of God. Just as your earthly identity has always been inextricably tied to your earthly parents, spiritual birth has given you a new Father in heaven. You are a child of the King – heir to all the rights, privileges and promises of being part of the royal family.

A new family

I remember, very clearly, a very important day in my life. That was the day my friend Ricky came home to his new parents just two houses up the block from me. It wasn't the typical homecoming of a new baby because Ricky was adopted at the age of four. There was a lot of commotion and I remember my mother saying something about '...they must have gotten a new child'. I had to check it out and to my delight found a new friend, just my age and just two houses away.

Since that time I have often thought what a wonderful thing adoption is. In Ricky's case he was given to an orphanage by someone who could not care for him and given a new life with people who wanted a child very much. Those were big changes for a four-year-old. He had to get used to having a father, mother and sister whom he had never seen, in addition to new surroundings and a new identity complete with a new last name.

It is not that different for a new-born Christian. The Christian is adopted by God (Eph. 1:5), given a new Father, given a new destiny, given new brothers and sisters – given a whole new foundation and approach to living. These are big changes and we have to get used to them, but these changes lie at the center of what it means for us to mature as Christians.[12] They are central to why we can leave the past behind. Let me give you three practical insights that will help you apply these truths.

Insight 1: God is my Father

I agree with those who say that we tend to view God the Father in the way we view our earthly fathers. I say this because I have seen it over and over again in counseling. We see it most in the subtle things like a general sense of emotional warmth or distance. If a person's father was kind he expects God to be kind. If a person's father was harsh he expects God to be disappointed easily. I saw this very clearly when I spoke with Pamela.

Pamela came to me because she just couldn't seem to 'get it together' in her Christian life. God didn't seem to be helping her change and grow like the Bible said she was supposed to. She explained how her mother had always been verbally abusive towards her. When Pamela was twenty-six instead of saying, 'Thank you for cleaning up my kitchen' her mother lectured her on how irresponsible she was to have put the toaster back in the wrong place after she had cleaned it.

I asked her about her dad and she spoke of him as a wonderfully kind and loving man who cared very much for her. I asked where he was when her mother would verbally attack her. She said he usually went into his room. 'Did he ever try to intervene on your behalf?' I asked. 'Yes,' Pamela said, 'but she would just turn on him and he quit trying.' Pamela was quick to say that after her mother finished yelling at her she would go to her room and cry, and her dad would come in and console her. I asked Pamela if she saw any connection between her father and God. She immed-iately pointed to her dad's love and concern as similar to God's love and concern. 'But your dad was incapable of helping you in the way you really needed it, by standing up to your mother,' I said. 'Yes,' she said with a curious look on her face, as she was wondering what I was getting at. Suddenly Pamela's eyes opened wide as she said, 'You're saying that just as my father was incapable of helping me with my problems with my mother I, deep down, don't expect God to be able to help me either. I know He loves me like my dad does, but He is incapable of really helping!'

Pamela, like all of us, had to learn to differentiate between her father and God in subtle things like expectations and power. The best way for us to do that is by getting to know our heavenly Father. Reading the Bible, especially Old Testament stories about His relationships with His people, is a must. Talk to Him. Not the same prayers you've always prayed, but really out pour your heart to Him about everything. Talk to Him as you read your Bible and watch Him guide your reading and meditation.[13] Finally, obey Him. Obey Him even when you don't feel like it or it is difficult. Obedience draws you closer to Him.

Insight 2: I am His child

I remember watching a television show when I was very young about a boy whose father was in prison. The neighborhood kids had given him such a bad time about being the son of a 'jailbird' that the boy began to believe what they were saying. He concluded that he was a 'bad seed' and would turn out just like his dad.

Many people fear that, and with good reason. As we have already said, we do tend to repeat the patterns we see in our parents. But whose child are you? If you are a Christian, you are a child of God. As His child you have a new heart and a new mind. You have the Holy Spirit living inside you, so by all means be like your Father – your heavenly Father! This is not sentimentality I am communicating. This is a present reality. You don't have to wait until heaven before you grow and change and leave your deepest pain behind. You are a child now and your Father in heaven wants to give you good gifts and teach you how to be like Him now.[14]

Insight 3: I have a new family

Two of the greatest gifts my parents ever gave me were my brother and sister. In spite of all the sibling squabbling that is a normal part of growing up, they have remained ever constant sources of strength and friendship. Just knowing I have relatives who bear my heritage is a comfort. I don't always agree with them nor they with me, but I know they are supportive and care. They are family and I can count on them.

When we come to Christ, our family tree really does branch out. No longer are we just part of our family of origin, but suddenly we are connected to every other Christian who has ever lived or ever will live. The importance of this is far reaching. We are never alone. Regardless of how our relationships are with our earthly families, we have another family with whom we will spend eternity that we can count on and draw strength from. Like any relationship it takes a while to build strong ties, but it is worth the effort. Jesus saw the new family as of such importance that He prayed for our unity the night before He went to the cross.

> My prayer is not for them alone. I pray also for those who will believe in me through their message, that all of them may be one, Father, just as you are in me and I am in you. May they also be in us so that the world may believe that you have sent me (John 17:20-21).

In the previous chapter I said that leaving yesterday behind means that we can be who we are in Christ. Our adoption into God's family (Eph. 1:5) secures not only our place in heaven but it assures us that God looks at us as His children now and He is ready to lavish on us all of the blessings that being His child guarantees.

A portrait of a born-again Christian

I am a person created in the image of God to reflect the character of my Creator. Although once broken and distorted through the sin of Adam and Eve, I am now a new person with a new capacity to grow and change and mature as a child of my heavenly Father. What a wonderful legacy He has left me. What a hero! He brought me back from the dead, gave me life – His life – and has told me to get out there and enjoy all the good things His Son purchased for me at the cross. What's more, He wants to get out there and enjoy life with me and all my brothers and sisters. He wants us to be a family. When there are problems, He's going to help us work them out. When there is work to be done, He's going to show us how to do it and then help us. What a great God! I want to grow up to be like my heavenly Father. How about you?

That's just the decision Jean made. Grace had empowered her to begin to live the Christian life in obedience to Christ regardless of her past. Now, understanding her new identity, she realized she was not trying to be a better version of her parents. She was to become more like her Father in heaven. What freedom she felt. What a relief!

Chapter 5

Learning to Change
Step 1: Taking Ownership

I have bought several used cars in my life. I realize the risk involved in buying a second-hand car. The previous owner may not have taken care of it. He may not be telling me all the problems with it. But once I buy it, it is mine for better or for worse. The car is my responsibility now.

Taking ownership of ourselves is important. I may not be responsible for what happened to me growing up, but I am responsible for what I do now. It might be much easier on the ego to blame others for our problems. If we can shift the blame, then we become victims and as a victim it is much easier to garner sympathy for our plight. But people who remain victims never fully mature.[15]

Is everything my fault?
Incidents such as being abused as a child, being beaten by a husband in a drunken rage, being physically maimed by someone's carelessness or being born to alcoholic parents are situations beyond our control. What we are responsible for is our response to the situations we are dealt.

Your reaction may be something like 'easier said than done', especially if you have suffered a severe injustice that has left indelible marks on you. That is understandable, but let me suggest that you may think it won't work for you because your expectations are different than God's. You look at it from the perspective of what you can do, God looks at it from the perspective of what He will do.

I wonder how we would complicate the matter of the woman caught in adultery in John 8 today? Would we send her for two years of intense therapy? Would we help her shift the blame on her parents and thereby say, in effect, 'With your past being what it was you couldn't help but become a prostitute'? Perhaps, but Jesus didn't. That's not to say that Jesus was unaware that the way a person is treated growing up affects their adult lives. It is to say, however, that at that point, what her parents did to her didn't matter. Jesus provided what she really needed: forgiveness for her sins and hope that she could change. He offers that to us as well.

Why we avoid responsibility

If it is so easy to receive God's forgiveness, why is there so much aversion to accepting our personal responsibility for our responses? I suggest, at least two reasons:

1. We think change is up to us. There is an important truth we must keep in mind, however; God does not command what He is not able, and willing, to provide the means to accomplish. He will encourage us along the way. The Holy Spirit indwells Christians and empowers them to live the life that is pleasing to God. We are involved in the changes that need to take place, but we are not alone. God is with us (Josh. 1:9; Phil. 1:6).

2. Another reason we avoid responsibility is that we lack the humility to say, 'I am at fault.' When Adam and Eve

were confronted, they attempted to shift the blame. Adam even suggested that God was somehow to blame because He gave Adam the woman who gave the forbidden fruit to him. Far too often we, like Adam, find some way to blame God for our own failings. We might not say it so blatantly, but if we are honest we will say we have in some way fallen in to this trap. We must be humble people, readily admitting our sins to a God who is able to forgive and help us.

Just what are we responsible for?

Does God expect you to know everything that's wrong with you and change right now? I like the illustration of the iceberg that Francis Schaeffer uses.[16] When we look at an iceberg what we see above the water is actually about a tenth of the whole iceberg. That means we don't see 90% of what is actually there. Dr. Schaeffer likens this to sin in our lives. What we see is only a small part of what is actually there. To carry the illustration even further let me ask the question, 'What if I were to shave off half of the 10% showing above the water? What percentage of the remaining iceberg would I be able to see?' The answer is still 10% because as I shave off the top more of the iceberg floats to the surface so there is always 10% showing above the water. So it is with sin. As I work, with the help of God, to overcome sin in my life I find that there is always more to work on. I have victory over one thing only to find there is a new thing, of which I was previously unaware. It is the process God has ordained to root out the sin in my heart. He doesn't overwhelm me by showing it all to me at once, but He does want it dealt with as it is revealed.

The question remains, 'Am I responsible for the whole iceberg right now?' I agree with Dr. Schaeffer that we are responsible to deal with sin in our lives as it appears but, and I must emphasize this, there is always something to deal with and work to overcome. We do not coast in the Christian life. There are times of relative calm as we work on things that are of less intensity than others, but there is always something. If there appears to be nothing we need to change in order to better conform to the image of Christ we must pray, as King David did:

> Search me, O God, and know my heart; test me and know my anxious thoughts. See if there is any offensive way in me, and lead me in the way everlasting (Psalm 139:23-24).

If we pray this prayer honestly, God will graciously show us what we need to work on to bring greater glory to Him.

I remember hearing a woman say that she was a flagrant violater of the speed limits, 'But', she said, 'God hasn't convicted me of it yet'. She knew it was wrong, but what she was really saying was, 'If I don't feel bad about it, it's O.K.' What I am saying is that there is always sin under the surface we don't see. We must respond to that portion we do see regardless of whether we feel guilty about it. If we know it is there we are responsible to deal with it.

What is God's attitude about sin?
He hates it. He also loves and understands us. So He extends His grace and gives us His Holy Spirit to work through sin step by step, bringing honor to Him and His plan every step of the way.

A major obstacle in my marriage has been closely related to this. I am a matter-of-fact person. When my wife was doing something that I thought she needed to work on I would say so. The problem was that when I said, 'You need to work to change this', she heard me saying something like, 'If this doesn't change right away I won't accept you and you are a failure.' I love my wife, and to me it was a very natural thing to point out what I knew she needed to know in order to grow. She, however, had not known anyone who could see her shortcomings and still love and accept her. Is that not the same struggle we have with God? God points out our sin because He loves us and wants us to conform to the image of His Son. We have difficulty taking God at His word. We know that God hates sin and we know that He demands satisfaction for the pain we have caused Him. What we so often fail to see is that God is fully satisfied through the death of Jesus on the cross. He no longer condemns those who are in Christ.

> Therefore, there is now no condemnation for those who are in Christ Jesus, because through Christ Jesus the law of the Spirit of life set me free from the law of sin and death (Rom. 8:1-2).

God accepts us and tells us of our sin, not to condemn us, but to help us grow to maturity. Conviction of sin is a very positive thing for the Christian because overcoming sin sets us free!

The buck stops here
Who is responsible for my life? As I stand before God I am the one who is judged for my own responses to life and the

situations in which I find myself. Others are judged for what they do, which may involve what they did to me, but I am held accountable for how I responded to their actions and to God.

Coming to grips with my personal responsibility and the fact that I can't blame anyone else for my failure to grow and change can be quite sobering, but also quite liberating. Knowing the truth frees me to follow the truth and therefore find freedom (John 8:31-32).

The issue of responsibility comes down to this: I am responsible to seek and surrender to the will of God in all that I do. No excuses, no blame shifting, just recognition of who I am and who He has created me to be in Christ.

Jean had felt anything but free growing up. She had believed that she was destined to be just like her parents and would never escape their domination. In a way she had believed that the only way to be free of them was to find a way to undo all the horrible things they had done to her. But the truth was coming through now. She would deal with her sin and God would deal with theirs. Her freedom would come not because she set herself free but because God set her free. She is not responsible for what they did – only her response to it. She could deal with herself, it was her parents she couldn't change. But to her delight she didn't have to! The question now was, 'Where do I start?'

Chapter 6

Learning to Change
Step 2: Taking Aim

To overcome a problem we must know what the problem is. That is not always a simple proposition. Sometimes we approach a problem and then find that it is only symptomatic of another, deeper problem. At other times we approach a problem only to find that it isn't really worthy of all the attention. I have known some people who dwell on certain 'safe' problems so they can avoid things that they really don't want to change. Finally, there are those who have a general uneasiness about life, but just can't seem to identify what, if anything, is wrong. How do we begin to work through this maze? As you might expect, God gives us principles in His Word to help.

In order to identify problems it is helpful to look at three major areas: the sins we have committed; the sins others have committed against us; the situations in our lives which have caused us pain.

Priority 1: The sins we have committed

'I just don't know why these things keep happening to me. I thought God was supposed to help me, but I keep having these problems and it is just not my fault.' The truth was that this young woman's problems *were* her fault. She had willingly violated the commands of God and was reaping the harvest many times over. What did she need to understand? That when we break the laws of God we pay a price.

> Do not be deceived: God cannot be mocked. A man reaps what he sows (Gal. 6:7).

Most of us accept the laws of nature. How often do we openly defy the law of gravity by walking off a tall building? Who do you know who challenges the laws of physics by remaining in the path of a speeding vehicle? Generally speaking, people are respectful of the natural laws of the universe. Why do we think that neglecting the laws of God would have any less severe consequences?

When we face problems we must first examine whether or not the problem, in full or in part, is our fault. Why do we start with self? Let's look at Matthew 7:3-5.

> Why do you look at the speck of sawdust in your brother's eye and pay no attention to the plank in your own eye? How can you say to your brother, 'Let me take the speck out of your eye,' when all the time there is a plank in your own eye? You hypocrite, first take the plank out of your own eye, and then you will see clearly to remove the speck from your brother's eye.

It is difficult to admit fault, especially if your role models rarely did. If we keep firmly in mind the principle from the last chapter, that the conviction of sin is a good thing because it allows us to receive forgiveness and overcome the problem, it can be a very positive aspect of our lives. David recognized in his own life how liberating a thing it is to have God forgive him.

For day and night your hand was heavy upon me; my strength was sapped as in the heat of summer. Then I acknowledged my sin to you and did not cover up my iniquity. I said, 'I will confess my transgressions to the LORD' — and you forgave the guilt of my sin. (Psalm 32:4-5)

God was very gracious to David by not allowing him peace until he finally confessed his sin. Did God know he had sinned? Certainly He did, but our relationship with God is a two-way relationship. Our confession is a way of showing that we take sin seriously, and it also serves as a way to cleanse our hearts before God and clear the way for continued relationship with Him. God takes this very seriously and so should we.

Where sin shows up: the physical

Earlier we looked at the verse from Galatians which says that we reap what we sow. The reaping of our sin may be manifest in many different ways. One way that we become affected is physically, with ailments such as heart disease, ulcers, headaches and other internal problems. The connection between sin and the physical shouldn't surprise us. We see it as early as Genesis 2:17 when God told Adam that if he ate of the forbidden fruit he would die (see also Rom. 5:12-21).

In Proverbs we are told that the fear of God and resistance to evil will give us good health.

Do not be wise in your own eyes; fear the LORD and shun evil. This will bring health to your body and nourishment to your bones (Prov. 3:7-8)

Having said what I have concerning the link between sin and physical ailments, we must strive for balance. All sickness is the result of the Fall of Adam and Eve, the effects of which have been passed on to us, but not all of our illness is the result of our own personal sin. Jesus makes this clear for us when addressed by His disciples:

> As he went along, he saw a man blind from birth. His disciples asked him, 'Rabbi, who sinned, this man or his parents, that he was born blind?' 'Neither this man nor his parents sinned,' said Jesus, 'but this happened so that the work of God might be displayed in his life' (John 9:1-3).

It is my desire that no-one reading this would be too quick to blame personal sin for their physical ailments. This is something we must be very careful about. Don't be too quick to be too hard on yourself. God will lead you through these and other problems as you trust Him to do so. If you think that your physical ailment is due to personal sin, the best way to deal with it is to get the help of a trusted counselor or friend. Let them help you sort out first, whether it really is a result of personal sin, and second, what to do about it. Any remedy will involve a spiritual change (repentance) and most likely a physical cure.

I have known many people who placed all the emphasis on the spiritual and neglected their physical health. People who, believing they had received forgiveness, threw away the pills they needed to control the physical ailments which may have been caused by the sin for which they received forgiveness. Both must be addressed because when sin has caused a physical ailment, we may be forgiven and remain physically ill. The man who has destroyed his body through alcoholism and then trusts in Christ, still has the effects of years of abuse. He is forgiven, and yet he needs medical attention. We must not neglect either the physical or the spiritual realities. Some find that what they thought were emotional problems were actually due to organic dysfunction. It is always a good idea to check with your physician to find out whether there is a physiological connection.

Where sin shows up: the soul

Another way we reap what we sow is in the area of emotional problems. The first glimpse we have of an emotional problem related to sin is, as you might have guessed, in the garden of Eden. When Adam sinned he experienced shame and fear for the first time (Gen. 3:10). Keep in mind why Adam and Eve experienced this breakdown in their emotional makeup. They were designed for obedience to God and when they tried to become what they were not designed for they experienced a malfunction. None of us were made to be autonomous. We all function properly when we are in the right, dependent relationship with our Creator. We must maintain what Cornelius Van Til refered to as the Creator-creature distinction. God is not man and man is not God and we must never confuse the issue.[17] The creature is to worship the Creator and not himself. Whenever we sin against God's divine commands we violate those principles by worshiping the desires of self which are in opposition to the desires of God.

The neglect of God's commands can lead to a number of emotional problems: fear, depression, anxiety, impotence, eating disorders, panic attacks, psychosis and the list goes on and on. When you face your emotional struggles, you must ask yourself whether it is the result of personal sin. Talk it over with a counselor or knowledgeable friend so that you don't jump to conclusions, but look at it seriously. It is important for you to repent if you are at fault.

This too is a process

Discovering whether our problems are our own fault is not always easy. There are, to be sure, those things that are easy to spot. Things like depression which is related to a lifestyle of adultery or drug abuse or intense lust in the person who is actively involved with pornography. Other things are not so easily spotted. I remember once working with a woman who was terribly hurt over her husband's years of insensitivity. As I worked with both her and her husband, what surfaced was an attitude in her that would not allow intimacy. For years she had accused him of being the problem so that she could avoid the vulnerability of a close relationship. This took some time to uncover. Some of your problems will also. Let me give you four hints to help you think through what is and is not your fault:

1. *Relax!* Don't be afraid of what you might find. If you do uncover some terrible fault, it will aid in your liberation as God breaks its power over you and you gain freedom from its tyranny.

2. The purpose of this exercise is to *produce freedom*, not guilt. Keep in mind that if you are a Christian, you are free from condemnation (Rom. 8:1).

3. *It may take some time*. Don't be discouraged if you have difficulty putting your finger on the problem. You may need a good biblical counselor to help you sort through things. Remember, some of the tougher problems you have to deal with took a long time in developing; they may take some time to uncover.

4. *Seek a high level of honesty in yourself*. Avoiding responsibility for your part in problems only perpetuates your discomfort and may actually serve to harden your heart further towards the repentance that will bring you freedom. Ask yourself the question, 'What wrong attitudes or behavior can lead to the type of problems I am experiencing?' It will help to pray as David did: 'Search me, O God, and know my heart; test me and know my anxious thoughts. See if there is any offensive way in me, and lead me in the way everlasting' (Psalm 139:23-24).

Priority 2: The sin committed against us

Some sin committed against us is obvious. Some is not so obvious as in Amelia's case.

Amelia's mother was one of those who would do anything for her husband and children. Washing clothes, making beds, cleaning dishes and cooking meals were all chores she thought she must perform to be a good mother and wife. The problem was that as she performed these services, she did so with a very negative spirit. It didn't stop with the housework, however. Amelia's mother had a very cynical outlook on most things. It was quite obvious that she did not enjoy life very much at all. She did what she was 'supposed' to do, but very begrudgingly. As Amelia grew up, she developed a similar attitude towards life and had the view that when people did things for her they did so out of duty but not love. This attitude took all the joy out of doing things for her family and attacked her own identity as a worthwhile child of God. Passing on a complaining spirit, even if it is a quiet, complaining spirit (seen through actions and body language rather than words) is as damaging as many more recognizable problems.

Getting to the root of the problem

To get to the root of what has been done to us we look for the obvious sin, then we look for the more subtle offences and thirdly we look at those things which are not really sins at all.

The obvious sins are those things which, unfortunately, we find in the news every day. Children who are neglected or abused physically, sexually or emotionally carry those scars with them for a lifetime. Adults who have experienced the trauma of unfaithfulness or spouse abuse or being lied to by people they trust share the struggle of overcoming difficult circumstances. There are far too many individual problems to list them all here. If you think you have been sinned against, use a good study Bible or topical Bible to help you identify where Scripture talks about your problem. As an example look at a famous 'list' of sins:

The acts of the sinful nature are obvious: sexual immorality, impurity and debauchery; idolatry and witchcraft; hatred, discord, jealousy, fits of rage, selfish ambition, dissensions, factions and envy; drunkenness, orgies, and the like. I warn you, as I did before, that those who live like this will not inherit the kingdom of God (Gal. 5:19-21).[18]

Did you grow up in an atmosphere of immorality, drunkenness, gossip? Were your parents selfish, jealous of what the neighbors could afford and they couldn't? Did you grow up listening to your mother for hours on the phone gossiping about other members of the church? If so, you have been affected in much the same way as if those things had been done to you personally. In a way they were, because your parents were called on by God to create a godly atmosphere in your home. To the extent that they did not they have sinned.

Identifying the sin committed against us is a process that may be painful, but it is necessary in order to know how to respond to our struggles. Keep in mind that although I have discussed the sin we commit and the sin committed against us in two different sections there is almost always some overlap. The reason is that we often respond to sin in a sinful manner. This is readily seen in the victim of child abuse, later abusing his own child. The daughter of an abusive father may respond in hateful, hurtful ways toward all men. The principle we have discussed already comes back in full force, 'I am not responsible for the sin committed against me but I am responsible for my response to it.'

The question we need to ask is, 'Regardless of what has happened in the past, what am I willing to do right now?' I am convinced that that is the question God most wants us to ask. He wants to know what we are willing to do right now.

The sin that is not sin

I have talked to many people who feel they have been wronged, yet when I pursue it with them find that the problem was more of a personal preference than a sin. All of us have been aware of churches that have split over such things as the color of the new carpet or whether or not an organ is used instead of a piano. These are things the Bible says nothing about, yet people elevate them to the status of orthodoxy. Most of us have preferences, but when we allow relationships to turn sour because we choose to take a stand over things God is silent about, we trivialize the things which really are important.

I knew a man once who was an excellent debater. He could present as convincing an argument for the authority of Scripture as anyone. The problem was he was just as adamant about which restaurant had the best Mexican food. In fact, he became known for being a man with opinions about everything. The fact that he would argue about Mexican food with the same intensity as defending Christianity served to trivialize both. We must learn what is worth fighting for and what is not. God doesn't call us to die for our preferences. He *may* call us to die for the sake of the gospel.

I'm spending time on this issue of preference because I have seen it destroy so many relationships. I remember hearing a noted Christian educator tell the story of a woman who wanted out of her marriage. When pressed to be specific about the kinds of things she just could not live with in this man, the infractions were quite trivial. Issues like the color of his pyjamas and the way he left the cap off the toothpaste were driving her to divorce, so she thought. She was in dire need of a reality check. The man's behavior may have been different from hers, but it was not sinful.

Perhaps you feel you were hurt by your parents in more subtle ways. You never got to spend the night with a friend or have friends welcomed in to your home. You may not have been allowed to attend school dances or other social occasions. A boy who lived next door to me had such a rigid schedule of house and yard work during the summer that school was a welcome relief. He had very little time for play and struggled to respect his father.

If you have suffered under such things, let me caution you. The exercise of preferences is not necessarily sinful if not prohibited in Scripture. Preferences may be sinful because of the motives behind them, but we must be careful about trying to read people's hearts. That is an exercise in which only God can participate. In areas where you suspect sinful motives, ask God to give you a heart to forgive and purpose not to repeat the same patterns yourself.

Priority 3: Situations which hurt us

Much of the personal pain we face in life is due to living in a fallen world and is not the direct result of a particular sin. Situations such as the death of a parent, death of a spouse or child, illness in ourselves or those we care about, poverty or other economic problems beyond our control and personal deficits such as a disability or our personal appearance may weigh very heavily on us. In all of these things we must identify the source of our struggle and seek the biblical solution, keeping in focus what is important in all of our struggles. We must strive to handle things in God's way for His glory. A word from Hebrews would be encouraging here:

Therefore, since we are surrounded by such a great cloud of witnesses, let us throw off everything that hinders and the sin that so easily entangles, and let us run with perseverance the race marked out for us. Let us fix our eyes on Jesus, the author and perfecter of our faith, who for the joy set before him endured the cross, scorning its shame, and sat down at the right hand of the throne of God. Consider him who endured such opposition from sinful men, so that you will not grow weary and lose heart (Heb. 12:1-3).

The identification of problems is essential. We must do our best to get to the root of the problem otherwise we may just re-arrange the branches without ever killing the tree. Once we have our problems in view it is time to come up with a plan to overcome the negative and replace it with the positive. After all, leaving yesterday behind is all about the work of Christ being applied to our lives in such measure that we look more and more like the people He wants us to be.

As Jean looked back over her life she identified several things which had affected her in a negative way. Her parents' drunkenness and verbal abuse were two recurring problems. She also recognized a general dread of the future probably related to their chronic negativism. Jean then took the courageous step of identifying her own sinful responses to these things. Among them were resentment, fear of the future and placing the opinions of her parents and others above the opinion of God.

Jean recognized that she had a lot of work ahead of her. Now that she was aware of the central issues she determined that with God's help she would face them head on.

Chapter 7

Learning to Change
Step 3: Taking Action

What is your attitude on this question of change? Change isn't easy, especially if the changes you need to make are some of the more difficult ones. If you do want to change, you can. God will help you. This chapter will help you put together a plan of action to take on problems and deal with them in a biblical manner. It is not a quick fix. It is a way of restructuring your life for growth that will last you a lifetime. A word of warning, however. To change in significant ways you must plan for change. The kind of change that transforms lives doesn't just happen. That transformation comes from having the right attitude, the right preparation and the right process to carry it through.

Change: the right attitude

As we travel the road of change, God tells us to love, trust and follow Him (Prov. 3:5-6; Mark 12:28-31). Once we are committed to the proposition that God is a good Father and He desires the best for us, then we are ready to set out on the course laid out for us in His Word by fully committing ourselves to Him and His methods for making us the people we should be.

There was a time in the life of Peter when he was asked some tough questions by the Lord Himself (John 21:15-19). Three times Jesus asked Peter, 'Do you love me?' Each time

Peter answered Him with increasing frustration that he did love Jesus. Jesus saw the need to test Peter because Peter needed to be certain himself that he was committed to Jesus no matter what. We find the reason in John 21: 18-19:

> 'I tell you the truth, when you were younger you dressed yourself and went where you wanted; but when you are old you will stretch out your hands, and someone else will dress you and lead you where you do not want to go.' Jesus said this to indicate the kind of death by which Peter would glorify God. Then he said to him, 'Follow me!'

The crux of the issue for Peter was, 'Do you love me enough to follow me all the way to the cross?' Peter was called upon to prove his love for Jesus many times. Peter did, in fact, follow Jesus all the way to death on a cross.

Do you have the right attitude to follow Jesus on the road of change? Tell Him you love Him and that you will follow Him. Then take the next step.

Change: the right preparation

Peter learned a lot about change. He learned that one who denied the Lord could be forgiven, strengthened and become a pillar of the church of Jesus Christ. He passed on some of what he learned in the two epistles that bear his name. In the first he says that what God wants of us is holiness and that to accomplish this holiness we must be always changing, always conforming to the character of Christ. He summarizes this method in 1 Peter 1:13:

Therefore, prepare your minds for action; be self-controlled; set your hope fully on the grace to be given you when Jesus Christ is revealed.

Following Peter's advice, there are three things we need to do if we are to change:

1. *Prepare our minds for action*. God wants us to think as He thinks. That way we will react properly when we are confronted with potentially harmful situations. A warm and mushy feeling about God is not enough. We must do the hard work to think like Christians. We must think biblically. This will not come without some serious study.[19]

2. *Be self-controlled*. Peter tells us that the Christian is to be self-controlled. The self-control he speaks of is regardless of how one feels. I may 'feel' like getting drunk when something bad happens. What I do, however, is to remain sober and deal with the problem with God's help (Eph. 5:18). Change takes personal discipline, but we are not alone. The Christian has the Spirit of God living within to encourage and guide him. *For God did not give us a spirit of timidity, but a spirit of power, of love and of self-discipline* (2 Tim. 1:7).

3. *Focus on the grace that will be ours when Jesus is revealed*. Sometimes our obedience seems dry and routine. We lack zeal for our mission. For this reason Peter tells us to focus on Christ's work for our salvation (1 Peter 1:13,18-21). Remembering how lost we were without Him, how different life is now and the glory to

come when He returns lifts our spirits and reminds us that all we do, no matter how mundane, has eternal meaning and benefits (Eccles. 12:13-14). Are you prepared for change? Whenever you think you are losing focus meditate on these things and get back on track.

Change: the right process

We come now to the 'how to' of change. This is the plan that will help put the process of change into motion. The apostle Paul instructs us in the process.[20]

> You were taught, with regard to your former way of life, to put off your old self, which is being corrupted by its deceitful desires; to be made new in the attitude of your minds; and to put on the new self, created to be like God in true righteousness and holiness (Eph. 4:22-24).

Paul tells us how to change by telling us to put off the old self, renew the mind and put on the new self. We'll look at each of these parts of the process.

Put off

If I no longer want to wear my coat I take it off. If I no longer want to 'wear' an attitude or behavior I need to take it off as well. Christians are to rid themselves of the habit of ungodly living in favor of Christ-like living in the whole of life.

The 'old self' is a person who has not come to Christ. This is a person whose motivation for living is self-centered. This person's outlook on life is habitual; he habitually looks at life from the perspective of self. His whole orientation is to think, act and feel as he always has. The Bible tells believers that this old self died on the cross and that we are to learn to live in the reality that our 'old self' is truly dead. What is left for the Christian is to allow this habitual way of life to die in favor of the new life that has been given.

I have heard stories about people who following the amputation of a limb have found that the sensation of the limb being there is very real. They may have the sensation of moving it and even having an itch. But there is nothing to move or scratch. After they have been without their limb for some time the sensation goes away and reality sets in. This serves as a good example for us with regard to spirituality. The old self is dead but what is left is the sensation that it is alive even though it no longer exists. As we grow in the reality that the old no longer exists and we live in the reality of the new, we lose the old sensation and instead appreciate the new reality. We are able to do this as we continue in this process.

Renewing the mind

We have been talking about change. The Bible calls it transformation.

> Do not conform any longer to the pattern of this world, but be transformed by the renewing of your mind. Then you will be able to test and approve what God's will is – his good, pleasing and perfect will (Rom. 12:2).

The Christian begins to see significant changes in his life as he begins to think biblically. Consistently thinking according to God's truth works within a person to bring his desires and actions into conformity with that truth. The mind is

renewed as the Holy Spirit works through the Word of God
to give the Christian the power to go on to the next step,
which involves putting something in the place of what you
have taken off. In mind renewal we search the Scriptures to
find the proper character trait, attitude or behavior to 'put
on' in place of the old habit.

Put on

Perhaps you or someone you know has struggled intensely
to overcome some habit. Maybe you are attempting to stop
the consumption of alcohol, yet you find yourself unable to
stop thinking about having a drink, and time after time give
in to the same old pressures. You tried to *put off* alcoholism
but were unsuccessful. Keep this in mind: *Whenever you
put something off you must put something on in its place.*
One reason we are unsuccessful in our efforts to change is
that we don't replace the negative with the positive. Let's
walk through a simple illustration of these principles.

Mitchell was a new Christian. Some of his new friends
confronted him about his habit of lying whenever he got in
a tough spot. Mitchell eventually understood from Scripture
that lying is wrong (mind renewal). Mitchell determined to
obey Scripture and stop telling falsehoods (put off). Next
he had to ask the question, 'How?' Like it or not Mitchell
just naturally thought of lying first, even when he didn't
have to. He needed to change his thinking, he needed his
mind renewed. To do this he studied what the Scriptures
teach about lying. He read the Old Testament stories about
people who lied and what happened to them. He asked a
Christian counselor about it and discovered that lying partly
stems from the desire to control other people. Mitchell found

that by lying he could keep people at a comfortable distance without ever exposing the real Mitchell. Mitchell was also confronted with the fact that it was going to be hard work to change his habit of lying. He was surprised by what the counselor told him to do to overcome his problem. What did the counselor tell him? Simply, to tell the truth (put on).

Mitchell began by identifying the problem and determining to overcome it (put off). He then learned how to think biblically about his problem (renewing the mind). Finally he replaced lying with truth-telling according to the Scripture (put on). Look at how simply Scripture puts it for us in Ephesians 4:20-32:

Put Off	Renew the Mind	Put On
Lying	Eph. 4:25	Truth-telling
Stealing	Eph. 4:28	Work and Share
Unwholesome Talk	Eph. 4:29	Exhort Others
Bitterness Anger	Eph. 4:31-32	Compassion and Forgiveness

Change involves all of life

Perhaps the first two verses of Ephesians 5 sum up the process of change best.

> Be imitators of God, therefore, as dearly loved children and live a life of love, just as Christ loved us and gave himself up for us as a fragrant offering and sacrifice to God (Eph. 5:1-2).

Change is conformity to the character of Christ. It isn't easy but it is possible. We must plan for it or it won't happen in the significant ways it needs to. If we will follow the truths of Scripture in co-operation with the work of the Holy Spirit in us, we will see ourselves grow in ways that will be beyond our expectations. But we have to want to change. We must quit playing the games we have been playing and admit that we have been holding on to these habits because they have become a security blanket, or because pleasing ourselves has been more important than pleasing God. We have to tell ourselves the truth and believe God's truth over and above all else.[21] We must trust God enough to obey Him.

The larger context for change[22]

So far I have spoken of change from the perspective of what individuals can do. That is very important. There is, however, a larger context that is just as important to growth. That is the context of the church, the body of Christ.

In our individualistic society many have treated the local church as an option.[23] Yet from the beginning of the book of Acts the local church had a primary function in the lives of believers. The writer of Hebrews admonished his readers not to neglect their gathering together (Heb. 10:25). Understood in context, the admonition was so that Christians would get the encouragement they need to persevere in the faith. The preaching of God's Word, the accountability of other believers, the worship of God, and partaking of the sacraments of the church are all means God uses to mature us in the Christian life.

Change will take place as we avail ourselves of the means God has given for change. A consistent relationship with a local body of believers who honor God and faithfully proclaim and apply His truth is an indispensable part of leaving yesterday behind.

Here is a quick check list for you as you consider structuring your life for change:

1. Have the right attitude. Commit yourself to Him and His process of change.
2. Identify the problem.
3. Find scriptural support. Find the different ways the problem is spoken of and illustrated in Scripture. Study these carefully.
4. Pray. Ask God to give you insight, right thinking, proper desires and the ability to do what you should.
5. Accountability. Get someone else, whom you trust, to pray for you and hold you accountable to change.
6. Come up with a plan that you can follow to achieve the goal of change.
7. Commit to the process even if you stumble. You will fall down along the way. You must get up, ask forgiveness, repent and go on towards your goal.
8. Don't neglect the other areas of your life. One area of change will be aided by the whole of life continuing 'on track' with God.

One issue Jean had to face was what to do when she was down. She recognized that when she felt that way it was easy to slide off into self-pity or depression. She used to go to alcohol when she felt that way, but not any more. Now she replaced the drinking of alcohol with reading and meditating on Scripture and taking special care to walk in obedience to God that day. When she felt down she read in Psalms or Proverbs. She also made devotional reading a part of every day. She would often comment on how what

she read in her morning devotions would prepare her for
something she would face that day. She knew that it was
more than coincidence.

Chapter 8

Anger

As we draw to a close in this section on the process of Christian growth there are three subjects that warrant special examination. These are anger, forgiveness and self-pity. I have never met anyone with significant problems in their past who did not struggle with these three issues. We will examine anger first.

The energy that anger produces can lead to great harm. That same energy can also be used to bring about great healing. For some, the problem with anger has been a lifelong struggle with many sad victims. Some have struggled for years with anger without knowing it. That is because anger comes in some deceptive disguises. One of the most common is depression. Other possible links are fear, anxiety, bitterness, resentment, fatigue, various illnesses, headaches, ulcers, vengeance, malice, and the list could continue. Anger does not arise out of the same situation every time. Anger can be passed on to children by parents through modelling. The children simply learn, by watching their parents, to express anger about things which aggravate them. It can also arise from fear, guilt, losses (such as death of a loved one, loss of control through victimization, loss of virginity, loss of health), unfulfilled expectations (in marriage, career, relationships), personal deficits (such as learning or physical deficiencies). Anger may also arise in any of these forms from lack of fulfilment in parent-child relationships.[24]

Whatever the cause of anger, our job is to determine when anger is warranted and when it is not. We must learn to deal with the negative and positive aspects of anger. When anger has become resentment or hate we must know what to do.

Not all anger is wrong

Although much anger does arise from negative circumstances we must assert that not all anger is wrong. In fact, sometimes it would be wrong not to become angry.

God, Himself, is sometimes angry (Psalm 7:11). He was angry with Solomon when Solomon's heart was turned away from the God he had loved (1 Kings 11:9). God was so angry with Israel that He removed the northern kingdom and it ceased to exist (2 Kings 17:18). Jesus showed this zealous anger towards the Pharisees (Mark 3:5).

Not all anger is right

'In your anger do not sin': Do not let the sun go down while you are still angry, and do not give the devil a foothold (Eph. 4:26-27).

From these short verses the apostle Paul says much about anger. One of the things he says is that not all anger is sin. He also tells us that anger which is not resolved quickly could become the foothold the devil needs to gain influence in our lives. To deal appropriately with anger we must first determine whether our anger is righteous or sinful and secondly what to do with it.

Righteous anger

How do we determine whether our anger is righteous or
not? Dick Keyes gives three aspects of anger to help determine its righteousness. According to Keyes, 'we need to
separate three aspects of anger. They are the cause, the
quality of the anger and the expression of it. If anger is to be
legitimate in the sight of God it must honor Him in all three
areas.'[25] Let us take a look at each of these areas.

Determining the cause of anger

The question of cause can be a difficult one. Motives are
hard to judge, even in ourselves. We must determine,
however, if our anger is primarily righteous or unrighteous.
Righteous anger will have the law of God in focus. When
Jesus became angry and chased the people out of the temple
it was out of a zealous concern for the principles of the
Father. When we face situations such as incest we know
from the Bible that such behavior is morally wrong and we
are right to be angry about it.

Sometimes the infraction is mixed with our own motives
of pride or jealousy and is not really sin on the other person's
part at all. These instances often arise from unfulfilled
expectations. Perhaps a man expects his wife to be punctual
or to have dinner prepared in a certain way. The husband is
angry and may be able to give a long discourse on punctuality
and the importance of a well-served meal, but this situation
does not warrant his anger. I can hear many men who would
retort, 'She knows how I want things and she just does this
to anger me.' Even if that is true, questions must be asked:
'Why does it anger you?' and, 'Even if she is trying to
aggravate you, why do you allow yourself to be enraged by

her behavior?' Think about it. If a wife is willing to do things she knows are going to hurt her husband, there is something wrong with her. The husband's response should not be self-serving, thinking about how awful things are for him. Rather, he should be concerned with his wife and seek to lead her in the direction of the Lord. She may be wicked or she may be ignorant of the proper way to relate to her husband. Either way her relationship with God is suffering and she needs to be called to account for the Lord's sake through the loving leadership of her husband.

Work hard to get at the causes of anger. Be honest enough to consider whether your anger is righteous. Keep in mind this rule: *If the Bible says it is wrong you may be angry for the Lord's sake. If it is not specifically prohibited in Scripture, be slow to anger.*

Be careful, because as soon as you determine that you have a right to be angry you run the risk of becoming involved in the sin yourself by responding in a sinful way. It is important to consider the quality of the anger.

Determining the quality of the anger

To determine the quality of the anger we must ask the question, 'Does the anger remain righteous or become sinful?'

If a girl is sexually abused by her father she has a right to be angry. If she becomes hateful or malicious she becomes part of the problem because she has responded to sin with sin. Some would say she not only has a right to be angry but she has a right to hate her father for what he has done. While we understand the hatred, it must be avoided. Consider the example of Christ Himself:

When they hurled their insults at him, he did not retaliate; when he suffered, he made no threats. Instead, he entrusted himself to him who judges justly (1 Peter 2:23).

Who more than Jesus had the right to be angry? Who more powerful than Jesus could have retaliated against those with whom He was angry? It is not that Jesus let anyone off the hook. It is just that He kept His perspective and entrusted them to the Father who was in a better position to deal with them. I am afraid that the reason we don't let go of anger by giving people over to God is the same reason Jonah did not want to go to Nineveh. We are afraid God will forgive them and we want them to pay for what they have done. Jonah's response to God's compassion on the people of Nineveh is convictingly honest:

But Jonah was greatly displeased and became angry. He prayed to the LORD, 'O LORD, is this not what I said when I was still at home? That is why I was so quick to flee to Tarshish. I knew that you are a gracious and compassionate God, slow to anger and abounding in love, a God who relents from sending calamity...' (Jonah 4:1-2).

We might not have the courage to articulate it so clearly, but perhaps if we could we might say exactly what Jonah did. Again, let me say that there are some things which happen to us or to people we love that warrant our intense anger but, as in all things, we must hold all things in God's perspective. If wrath is warranted no-one can match the fierce wrath of God. On the other hand, if God chooses to have compassion on them (as He has on us), who are we to get in the way?

Righteous anger focuses on the wrongness of the evil done rather than on the destruction of the person doing it. If our anger is going to remain righteous we must maintain our focus on the things of God.

The expression of the anger

1. Anger is to be under control

'He hurt me.'

'Physically?' I asked.

'Yes. He threw me out of the room.'

Julie was angry, but more than that she had been deeply wounded. Her husband had become angry and responded in frustration. I asked Logan, Julie's husband, what had happened. He had been working in the study and she had come in to ask a question about dinner. In the brief conversation that took place a hot button was pushed and Logan became angry and threw her out of the room. I asked him why he reacted as he did.

'When she does that,' he glared, 'I can't help but get her out of my sight.'

'You can't help it?' I asked.

'No, I can't,' he replied.

'Do you mean to say that you are out of control at that point?' I inquired.

'Yes. She makes me so mad, I just can't help it.'

I pushed a little harder and asked, 'Are you saying that she takes control of you?'

'Yes!' he replied with a little anxiety in his voice. 'You don't know how angry it makes me when she does that.'

I pushed still harder, 'If you are out of control and not responsible for what you do to her, shouldn't you be locked up to protect both your wife and yourself?'

Logan settled back, beginning to realize what I was getting at, and said, 'No, I'm not out of control like that.'

As we talked Logan began to understand that no-one *makes* him angry, he chooses to respond in anger. He also realized that he could not so easily use anger as an excuse for his behavior.

The apostle Paul recognized that anger was controllable.

'In your anger do not sin': Do not let the sun go down while you are still angry (Eph.4:26).

According to Paul a person can be angry without letting it go too far. That person can also determine to bring resolution to their anger in a certain period of time. This tells us a great deal about our relationship to anger. We are in charge of it! Anger is not to control us. This is how Jesus related to anger in the temple courts. He was in control yet He was intensely angry. When He saw the Father's house being turned into a market He made a whip and drove people and cattle out. He was in control. He took the time to make a whip, He chased the people out and He spoke intelligent words to them. He was not in a blind rage but He was filled with anger which was kept in perspective. He directed His anger at the problem and found a way to resolve the problem. In this case He resolved it by closing the market.

2. Anger's expression should be of short duration
So that it does not turn into resentment, anger must be

resolved quickly. While Stephen was being stoned he prayed for God to forgive the sin of those stoning him. Jesus had done the same thing on the cross. The episode in the temple we have just looked at was quick and to the point. We must strive to take care of anger as quickly as possible by directing it at a righteous solution to the problem in hand.

3. Anger is sometimes directed at institutions which are evil

Jesus took on the Scribes and Pharisees as a whole, yet was a friend to individual Pharisees. There are some institutions which warrant our anger, yet we must maintain Christian character in dealing with them.

4. Anger is corrective

Anger should be aimed at helping to correct the situation. As Christians we are often called on to do the opposite of what might come naturally to us as humans. When the world might use a situation to destroy someone, Christians are called to heal and restore. Paul expressed it well:

> Do not repay anyone evil for evil. Be careful to do what is right in the eyes of everybody. If it is possible, as far as it depends on you, live at peace with everyone. Do not take revenge, my friends, but leave room for God's wrath, for it is written: 'It is mine to avenge; I will repay,' says the Lord. On the contrary: 'If your enemy is hungry, feed him; if he is thirsty, give him something to drink. In doing this, you will heap burning coals on his head.' Do not be overcome by evil, but overcome evil with good (Rom. 12:17-21).

There is a righteous way to deal with anger. It is to use anger and its energy to attack the problem constructively rather than self or others. This approach looks at the wrong done by someone and confronts that person's behavior with a view toward lovingly correcting them and resolving the hurt incurred. Anger, so directed, must be in keeping with Christian character as commanded by Christ (Matthew 5–7) and must be solution-oriented.

If you are someone who has not dealt with anger properly you need to understand how your persistent anger affects your relationship with God.[26] It affects your prayer life (1 Tim. 2:8); the ability to lead (Titus 1:7); guidance from God (1 John 2:10-11); and assurance of salvation (1 John 3:15).

Unrighteous anger may show itself in foolishness (Prov. 12:16), sinful thinking (1 John 2:10-11), lack of control (Prov. 29:11) and lack of relationships since people won't want to be around you (Prov. 22:24-25). It affects your relationship with God, yourself and other people. It may affect your health and lead to activity which could cost you your life. Anger will always find expression. One way or another unresolved anger will show itself.

Dealing with anger

The wrong way to deal with anger

There are several unrighteous ways people have tried to express their anger. I will look briefly at four.

1. *Venting our anger*. Anger is released towards others or a situation with little control. Some hit walls or pillows or other people or go into a screaming tantrum. Proverbs warns against such an inappropriate response.

A fool gives full vent to his anger, but a wise man keeps himself under control (Prov. 29:11).

2. *Anger is turned inward.* Clamming up and internalizing anger may result in a person becoming bitter and resentful and perhaps depressed. Often people are so afraid of getting a response they don't want they would rather remain quiet than confront the situation.

3. *Anger is directed at a substitute.* A man may be angry at his employer but rather than direct his anger at the problem he goes home and expresses anger towards his wife and children. Scripture is clear, however, that we are to speak the proper word to the proper person.

Do not let any unwholesome talk come out of your mouths, but only what is helpful for building others up according to their needs, that it may benefit those who listen (Eph. 4:29).

4. *Denial.* Anger is suppressed and the problem is not recognized. Scripture tells us not to deny our sin but to recognize it truthfully and deal with it righteously. 'In your anger do not sin...' (Eph. 4:26).

The right way to deal with anger
To resolve anger righteously we must keep several things in focus.

1. *Face it honestly.* When we are angry we must call it anger without disguise. Some people live years with continuous problems because they are unwilling to admit their anger.

2. *Own the anger*. When anger is discovered we must take responsibility for dealing with it.

3. *Determine to resolve it God's way*. This involves thinking it through to determine whether or not it is righteous or unrighteous anger. Honesty is a must. Remember that the important thing is not who is at fault but whether God is honored by the resolution of it.

In your anger do not sin; when you are on your beds, search your hearts and be silent. Selah (Psalm 4:4).

Honest introspection is a good thing if it is for the purpose of pleasing God. We stand in grace. We need not fear finding out something is our fault. God's forgiveness is sure for those who confess their sin (1 John 1:9). The focus must be on resolving the anger God's way.

4. *Determine to catch it at the kindling point*.

My dear brothers, take note of this: Everyone should be quick to listen, slow to speak and slow to become angry (James 1:19).

Starting a quarrel is like breaching a dam; so drop the matter before a dispute breaks out (Prov. 17:14).

Catch it early and it is much easier to deal with. It's like debt. If we deal with our debt when there is a little of it, it is not so overwhelming. If we wait too long the burden is heavy and we are tempted to run away from it. Keep short accounts of anger.

5. *Be quick to forgive.*

Be kind and compassionate to one another, forgiving each other, just as in Christ God forgave you (Eph. 4:32).

Withholding forgiveness hurts everyone. More about this in the next chapter.

6. *Love one another as Christ loves us.*

Above all, love each other deeply, because love covers over a multitude of sins (1 Peter 4:8).

Love is patient, love is kind. It does not envy, it does not boast, it is not proud. It is not rude, it is not self-seeking, it is not easily angered, it keeps no record of wrongs (1 Cor. 13:4-5).

Love does cover a multitude of sins. If you are caught up in the anger cycle, ask God to give you a heart of compassion towards those with whom you are angry. If the person you are most angry with is yourself, ask God for a heart of compassion to deal with yourself as well. If your anger has been present for some time and it has become resentment, you must deal with the resentment first.

Dealing with resentment

Do not be quickly provoked in your spirit, for anger resides in the lap of fools (Eccles. 7:9).

It is easy to be a fool in the sense that Solomon points out. It is easy because it feels so good. It feels right to hold on to our anger because the person we're angry with does not deserve our forgiveness. That is, after all, what resentment is – *unforgiveness*. If we are going to get serious about growing in Christ we must leave behind any thought we have of holding on to resentment. Here are five points to take us through the process of dealing with resentment.

1. *Confess it as sin*. God says anger is to be dealt with quickly. If we have held on to it we must confess our own sin of not trusting God and obeying Him.

> He who conceals his sins does not prosper, but whoever confesses and renounces them finds mercy (Prov. 28:13).

2. *Gain God's perspective*. God's answer to resentment is mercy. Mercy on God's part towards you and mercy on your part towards the person you are resenting.

> But love your enemies, do good to them, and lend to them without expecting to get anything back. Then your reward will be great, and you will be sons of the Most High, because he is kind to the ungrateful and wicked. Be merciful, just as your Father is merciful (Luke 6:35-36).

3. *Forgive the person for whom you hold resentment*. Imitate your heavenly Father's attitude towards you and have mercy toward the person you resent.

4. *Seek the forgiveness of those you have resented.* If this is not possible because of death, or if for some reason you cannot contact them, be certain before God that you possess an attitude of forgiveness.

> Therefore, if you are offering your gift at the altar and there remember that your brother has something against you, leave your gift there in front of the altar. First go and be reconciled to your brother; then come and offer your gift (Matt. 5:23-24).

5. *Act upon your forgiveness through acts of mercy.* If you can begin to see people through God's eyes you will begin to have compassion on them. Since they are people who do such terrible things as they did to you, just think how sad their lives must be. When you love that person you begin to experience some of what it means to be like Christ. He gave to people who should have given to Him. He gave even to the point of giving His life for people who, at the time, hated him (Rom. 5:8).

> '...If your enemy is hungry, feed him; if he is thirsty, give him something to drink. In doing this, you will heap burning coals on his head.' Do not be overcome by evil, but overcome evil with good (Rom. 12:20-21).

God's answer to resentment is different than the world's. God's perspective has in focus the character of Christ and the healing of the one who is resented. He also has in focus what is best for us. It is always best for us to put anger and resentment behind us and get on with the main purpose of our lives. Focusing on the main purpose of life is possible because Jesus has broken the stranglehold of sins making it possible for us to replace anger with love and resentment with forgiveness.

Resolving anger will involve a re-affirmation of your own position in God's grace and your willingness to forgive, which we discuss in more detail next.

Chapter 9

The Dynamics of Forgiveness

Those of us who know Jesus Christ as our Lord and Savior know something of what it means to be forgiven. If we have grown in our Christian lives and studied God's Word we have an ever-increasing awareness of the depth of our sin and the depth of His forgiveness. We should, if we don't already, understand that God's forgiveness is based upon His character as a merciful God and upon the work of His Son applied to us. God's forgiveness is by His grace. We did not earn it. In fact, Christ died for us when we were in rebellion against Him (Rom. 5:8). In Romans 3 Paul makes it very clear how awful a people we were that Christ died for. In Psalm 51 David pours out his heart to God after his sin with Bathsheba. David is aware of how deeply he is in need of God's mercy and restoration.

We are a people who are in need of God's forgiveness. We needed it to become Christians and we need it to continue in the Christian life. That is not all we need, however. While we need to have hearts that are forgiven we also need to have hearts that forgive.

Who should forgive?
Jesus intended for those whom He forgave to themselves be forgiving people. Whatever we have suffered at the hands of other people Jesus suffered it first (Heb. 2:5-18; 4:14-

15). So close is the relationship between our being forgiven
and our forgiving that Jesus based one on the other.

> For if you forgive men when they sin against you, your
> heavenly Father will also forgive you. But if you do not
> forgive men their sins, your Father will not forgive your
> sins (Matt. 6:14-15).

Also the apostle Paul in Ephesians 4:32 writes:

> Be kind and compassionate to one another, forgiving each
> other, just as in Christ God forgave you.

The message is that those of us who have experienced God's
forgiveness will be people predisposed to forgiving. That is
not to say it is always easy but we will, with God's help, be
able to forgive those who have wronged us.

Why forgive?

First, because God demands that we forgive as we have been
forgiven. When we forgive we imitate the character of our
Lord.

Second, we forgive for the purpose of restoring the other
person to a position of relationship with us and with God.

> If anyone has caused grief .... The punishment inflicted
> on him by the majority is sufficient for him. Now instead,
> you ought to forgive and comfort him, so that he will not
> be overwhelmed by excessive sorrow. I urge you,
> therefore, to reaffirm your love for him (2 Cor. 2:5-8).

Forgiveness re-establishes a relationship as the person wronged grants that forgiveness as Christ forgave him.

How often must I forgive?

Some may ask how often should you forgive someone who continues to sin against you. Jesus was asked that same question and replied by saying:

> 'If your brother sins, rebuke him, and if he repents, forgive him. If he sins against you seven times in a day, and seven times comes back to you and says, "I repent," forgive him' (Luke 17:3-4).

The point is that we are to continue to forgive. I have wondered what the purpose would be in forgiving a person so many times. If the person continues to hurt you and then asks forgiveness, they must not be sincerely sorrowful, yet we are told to forgive. I would like to offer two reasons we forgive this person beyond what has already been stated above.

First, our forgiving, based simply on a person asking, keeps us out of the business of trying to determine their motives. We cannot read a person's heart so we shouldn't try. Only God knows people's hearts and we must leave Him to deal with them if they are not truly repentant. If they are truly repentant our forgiveness of them will clear the way for their restoration, which brings me to my second point. Forgiving people not only frees them but it also frees us. It frees us from resentment and bitterness and from seeking revenge. Forgiving allows us to leave the past behind and get on with the life God desires for us.

Who should be forgiven?

This is a tricky, and somewhat controversial, question which must be answered in two ways.

First, God calls me to have a heart of forgiveness towards anyone who sins against me. Notice I said 'who sin'. I am not talking about people who annoy us. If we are offended because of our preferences being stepped on that is not something for which we need to forgive. We probably need to broaden our attitudes and just not be so picky (there may be an issue of pride which we need to confess since being picky arises from an arrogant sense that life should be the way I say it should be). If some principle of Scripture is violated, my attitude should be that of Stephen who prayed for those who were stoning him and asked that God would forgive them.

Second, although we should have a heart of forgiveness towards those who wrong us, that is not to say that we verbally forgive those who do not ask for it. I have already said that we forgive in our hearts anyone who sins against us, but we have to be careful about saying, 'I forgive you', to those who have not asked for it. If they do not recognize their sin, forgiving them, as far as they are concerned, is meaningless and it could keep them from seriously confronting their own behavior.

I remember confronting someone once who refused to admit he had done anything wrong but ended the discussion by saying, 'You're suppose to forgive me anyway.' When I asked him, 'Forgive you for what?', he just said, 'For anything I've done wrong,' yet he still refused to say he had done anything wrong. I had to let him know that until he confessed something specific I could not grant him forgiveness verbally and the relationship would suffer. That is not to say I became bitter because I did forgive him before God, but in regards to our relationship there was still a barrier. People need to confess their sins to each other just as God wants us to confess to Him so that the air can be cleared and the relationship restored.

Do I have to like people I forgive?

Henry was starting a business which was full of promise. He asked his friend George to invest a substantial amount of money which he promised to pay back with interest at the end of a year. When the end of the year came Henry asked George if he would like to keep the money in the company and receive interest checks quarterly. George declined, explaining that he wasn't interested in investment, just in helping Henry get started and he would rather have his money returned with the year's interest according to the original agreement. Henry said he did not have the cash to pay him but would like to begin monthly payments to pay it back over the next year. George felt 'stuck' and agreed to the new arrangement.

The months went by and no payments came, so George contacted Henry who apologized and told of his bad luck with some business deals but assured George that payments would start up right away. They never did. Henry always apologized and made promises but never delivered on those promises. George even offered to cut the interest in half just to get it over with. Still no payments came. Henry was always 'very sorry' but never asked for forgiveness and never resolved his debt.

Here is the dilemma for George. As a Christian he knows

he must forgive Henry, but does that mean he has to continue their friendship as though there is not a problem? I firmly believe the answer is no. Forgiving someone does not mean that the consequences of sin are removed. In Henry's case George should follow the principles of Matthew 18 which would involve confronting him personally, then with someone else, and if he still does not repent he should be taken before the elders of the church if he is a Christian. If Henry is not a Christian or refuses to go before the elders then the civil courts may be appropriate. Obviously George could no longer respect Henry but he had to maintain Christian character in dealing with him. That means he couldn't gossip about him nor could he grumble and complain to others about the situation. Instead he had to give the matter over to the proper authorities, forgive him before God and pray for Henry's restoration. He did not have to respect Henry and certainly should never enter into a financial relationship with him again.

What if Henry were to come to George and, showing great remorse, ask for his forgiveness? Let's say that George is very humble and is delighted to see a sinner repent and grants Henry forgiveness. Does that mean the past is blotted out and that George should not require Henry to pay off the debt? He could handle it in that way, but he certainly is not required to. If Henry's remorse is real, his concerns are not the debt but the pain inflicted on George, his own violation of God's commands and the dishonor and pain he has brought to the heart of God. Just because George forgives him does not mean that he cannot still require Henry to pay the debt in full. Repaying the debt should be what Henry wants to do anyhow.

I have taken the time to give the above example because it is so common. There is a school of thought in the evangelical community which tells us that when we forgive it is as though the infraction never happened. That is just not true. If it were, Adam and Eve would still be in the garden of Eden. Although God had mercy on Adam and Eve, He still held them responsible and required them to leave the garden and eventually suffer physical death.

No, forgiveness does not mean we have to start respecting someone who is not respectable. It does mean that we have to live in such a way as to no longer be burdened with that person's infraction. It is not that we forget it; we can't. What we do is defer judgment to God who always judges fairly. I say, in effect, 'God, I have been sinned against. Your Word confirms that what this person did was wrong. Father, I also know that you forgave me when I sinned against you and that you, in turn, ask that I show this person the same grace you have shown me. I trust you to deal properly with this person so I give them to you, I forgive them, and I ask you to help me put this behind me and get on with the great purpose for which you have called me.'

What about hard-to-forgive cases?

Forgiving when both of you have sinned
In this case you must humble yourself and go to the person and confess your sin. If the person participated in this sin with you, he or she should be asking your forgiveness too but may or may not. You have the responsibility to confess your sin to the person (Matt. 5:23-24) and to confront him or her concerning his or her sin as well (Matt. 18:15-17).

This does require a great deal of humility and tact, otherwise it will appear that you are blaming your behavior on the other's and you must never do that. Sometimes it is best to confess your sin and ask for forgiveness and talk to the person about his or her part in it at another time. It is possible that the person will not accept your confession because to do so would mean he or she had sinned too. In this situation you must make your case from Scripture and encourage the person to confess as well so that he or she may enjoy restored fellowship with God.

Forgiving when they do not admit fault

A situation comes to mind where a young couple engaged in sex out of wedlock. Distraught, the young man went to the woman confessing that it was wrong and asked her forgiveness. She took the opportunity to let him know he was to blame and that she did not want to have anything more to do with him. The woman was just as responsible as the man yet he was the only one who confessed. He could leave there knowing he had done the right thing. While his relationship with the woman was not restored, since she did not grant forgiveness nor did she ask for forgiveness, his relationship with God was restored because he did what God said he should do.

We are responsible to let others know if they have sinned against us, but we are not responsible for what they do with the information. When we find ourselves in those situations in which we are willing to be humble but the other person is not, we must do the right thing ourselves and leave the other person in the Lord's hands. Sometimes he or she will eventually come around, but even if the person does not

God has been honored by our obedience and that is of central importance.

Forgiving those who have done us great harm

Issues that are very much in the news these days, such as childhood sexual abuse, alcoholism, physical and verbal abuse, require special attention. These are the situations which are often so difficult to forgive because the dynamics of victimization are so complex. For example, a woman who was sexually abused by her father as a child often experiences a sense of guilt because she thinks that she did something to deserve it or encourage it. There must be a clear sorting out of what was truly our fault and what was not. Once we understand that someone else hurt us deeply, the anger is often so intense that we run the risk of dealing with it in an inappropriate way. We must follow the clear teaching of Scripture concerning confrontation and resolution of these things. If you are someone who has experienced tragedy of this sort let me encourage you to get help from a pastor, biblical counselor or a trusted friend who understands the Bible, so you will know what needs to be said and when to say it. While we need to deal with things quickly, we also need to take the time to approach it with all wisdom. Take some time to learn the proper approach in your situation.

What about 'repressed' memories?

It is popular today for therapists to 'unlock' the memories within a person's subconscious which are so painful that they have been suppressed, sometimes for many years. It may be the rape of a woman by her father or some other atrocity. It is beyond the scope of this book to discuss this in detail but a few comments might be helpful.[27]

First, it is important to note that while there have been many who have claimed to discover things of this nature hidden away in their minds, there are also those who have been falsely accused at the suggestion of a therapist or misinformed friend. Keep in mind that living the Christian life and enjoying the blessing of God is not dependent upon your past, good or bad. It is based upon your relationship with God in the present.

Second, if there is something that you do not remember and it is important for you to remember, God will let you know as you pursue life in Him. A woman I worked with told me of a memory of a man walking into her room at night. He wore her Daddy's boots but she could never 'see' his face. She associated great distress and a sense of moral filth with the memory and wondered whether it was her father molesting her. I told her that I did not know. But what I did tell her brings me to my third point, which is that even if he did molest her, God would give her the grace to forgive him. That is the point we must recognize. Forgiveness is the real 'value' in remembering anything so horrible. For in forgiveness we release a person to the justice of God and we release ourselves to pursue the love of God without being embittered. But the sense I get from pop-psychology is that people need someone to blame. We do not need to blame, we need to forgive. It is in forgiveness for great personal atrocities that we most exhibit the character of Christ.

You have heard that it was said, 'Love your neighbor and hate your enemy.' But I tell you: Love your enemies and pray for those who persecute you, that you may be sons of your Father in heaven (Matt. 5:43-45a).

Why we forgive

We forgive because God forgives. Forgiveness is not an option for the Christian, it is a way of life. As we have seen there are many reasons we don't forgive, but there are no excuses for not forgiving. It is not always easy and sometimes it comes at great personal cost in the sense that we have to let go of resentment that has been the cornerstone of our lives for years. People who hate get a great deal of energy from that hate. It becomes a way of life (as can any emotion which takes control of us and becomes the centre of our existence). Replacing hate with love, however, is what God desires and the energy that comes from loving is much more pleasing to the Father and much more productive for the kingdom of God.

Receiving forgiveness

Lloyd was angry. He had been angry for several years. He was angry towards his father for being so hard on him while he was growing up. He was angry at his mother for standing by and allowing his father to hurt him with his harsh, demeaning words. Lloyd was also angry at his high-school friend for drawing him into activities he knew were wrong. Most of all, Lloyd was angry at himself. He knew better, he should have been stronger. As a result of these experiences Lloyd suffered a deep sense of guilt and came to a saving knowledge of Jesus Christ. Through his relationship with Christ, Lloyd was able to forgive his parents for the things they did to him while he was growing up. He forgave his friend and was instrumental in helping him find a new direction in life. Yet, long after Lloyd had made peace with his parents and his friend, he still could not receive the forgiveness of God. 'After all,' he thought, 'I knew it was wrong, I should have been stronger.'

I have known many Lloyds; people who grew up with expectations of near perfection in all things and who were treated very harshly when they blew it. They grow up to be people who, in the absence of their parents, take the place of their parents in being harsh on themselves. God has a better way. It involves having the humility to accept that I am not good enough or strong enough to meet God's perfect standard in my own strength. It also requires a changed attitude towards receiving and living God's forgiveness.

The Bible tells us that God forgives so that we can further conform to the image of Christ. If we are forgiven it is to free us to serve God, not to give us further license to sin (See Galatians 5:16-17 and 1 Peter 2:16).

There are at least two problems here which are closely related. First is that we don't understand the forgiveness of God, and second that we don't understand the basis of the forgiveness of God.

The forgiveness of God
The forgiveness of God is based, not on His duty to forgive us, for He has no obligation to do so, but on His love. 'For God so loved the world that He gave His Son...' (John 3:16). What God did with our sin was not to ignore it, but to put it on Jesus so that its wages would be paid off in His death (Rom. 6:23). Jesus was willing to do this (John 10:18). Dick Keyes has said: 'When wrong is done, someone must absorb the loss if there is to be reconciliation. Otherwise there will be a stalemate or endless cycle of retaliation and revenge. Jesus has absorbed the loss for our sin, taking our punishment

on Himself. This is not because of anything excusable in us, but simply because He has loved us enough to forgive us.'[28] What God says is, 'Forgiven is forgiven.' What God no longer condemns is not condemned, and that includes us (Rom. 8:1).

The basis of our forgiveness

To receive forgiveness we don't need to approve of what we have done or even 'come to peace with it'. The things we have done may indeed be detestable, but the basis of forgiveness is not feeling good about the sin or sinner. The basis is the love of God, your love for Him and His love for you. God loves us and we must accept and live in His forgiveness (John 8:31-36; Rom. 5:8,11).

Getting off easy?

Part of the problem with receiving the forgiveness of God or others reflects the view that if I am forgiven I am being let off the hook too easily. That's not quite true. It is true that when we accept the grace of God we are getting life when we deserve death, but it is not accurate to look at it as though some sin were being overlooked. God paid for our sin with the death of His Son. Our forgiveness is purchased in the same way as the forgiveness of anyone. It was purchased with the death of Jesus. His death was sufficient to cover all sin and it came at a great price.

A final word

Before we leave this topic I must refer to something discussed in an earlier chapter. We may have trouble receiving forgiveness because forgiveness means leaving condemnation behind, and many of us are so accustomed to self-condemnation or what we perceive to be God's condemnation, that we would feel lost without it. To be forgiven is a change in our thinking. It means I must now live as forgiven. God wants us to humble ourselves and then walk in obedience to Him. One of those acts of obedience is to no longer entertain thoughts of self-condemnation or the condemnation of God since He has declared us forgiven in Christ. If we are not to live in condemnation, what would He have us do? Perhaps the prophet said it best:

> He has showed you, O man, what is good. And what does the LORD require of you? To act justly and to love mercy and to walk humbly with your God (Micah 6:8).

By breaking the stranglehold of sin Jesus has secured for us the basis on which we are forgiven and the basis on which we can forgive.

Jean was surprised. Her surprise came when she discovered how ready and willing she was to forgive her parents. No, they didn't admit they had done anything wrong. But Jean forgave them in her heart before God. She had been so hurt and full of resentment that she had not realized how much she cared about them. Now when she saw them she no longer did so in hopes of gaining their approval. She went to them now as a missionary in hopes that she could show them the hope and mercy God had shown her. Jean no longer feared them, she loved them with God's merciful love.

Chapter 10

Avoiding Self-pity

When we think about tragic circumstances in our lives some people feel down, even depressed. When we have experienced suffering it is easy to get wrapped up in our circumstances and the resulting damage done in our lives. In some situations it is even proper to grieve. The loss of childhood, for example, due to sexual abuse is, in some ways, like a death over which we grieve. The child died in that he or she was forced into adulthood far too early at the hands of someone whom he or she trusted. Sometimes it is proper to grieve and to hurt over the condition of the world or the things done to us. What we have to avoid, however, is the paralysis of self-pity. We may be sad with good reason but if we give in to self-pity we allow the person or situation that hurt us to control us.

Self-pity comes when we are overwhelmed by how circumstances affect us. We may become irrational, emotional, depressed, angry or all of the above. When someone is involved in self-pity he does not have God's perspective because he is so concerned with what is happening to him he forgets to see the whole picture. Such was the case with Asaph.

Asaph: perspective lost

Asaph, the writer of Psalm 73, was like many of us. He looked around him and saw prosperous people who did not fear God. I can imagine that some of the people he saw prospering were those who had hurt him in some way. Perhaps they took unfair advantage of him in business or hurt his family. Whatever the case, as Asaph looked at their prosperity and his own discouragement he came close to despair.

But as for me, my feet had almost slipped; I had nearly lost my foothold (Psalm 73:2).

This was a man who was almost over the edge. He was a godly man but he made a terrible mistake. When he faced trials in his own life he started looking at the people who were not godly and sought to judge his own situation by theirs. When he did this his heart became polluted.

For I envied the arrogant when I saw the prosperity of the wicked (Psalm 73:3).

Envy entered his heart when he lost sight of the fact that his situation was different from theirs. His perspective was to be God's, but he was sharing the perspective of the world. That is usually the case when we are struggling. At the time we most need to look at life through the eyes of faith we start thinking like the world does. Asaph was caught in this trap. The heart of self-pity is envy and Asaph was envious; envious of the prosperity he saw among people whom he did not think were worthy of it.

Asaph's loss of perspective did not involve only monetary success. He saw the wicked as prospering in many ways. Asaph observed that they were healthy, strong and free of struggles and other common burdens of the day (vss. 4-5). Beyond that he saw them getting away with things that others would not; things like arrogance, conceit, violence and oppression (vss. 6-9). Then to make things worse other people in the community looked to these wicked people with admiration (vss. 10-11). This was too much for Asaph to take and it is at this point in the psalm that he indulges in the height of self-pity, questioning the value of his own obedience to God.

Surely in vain have I kept my heart pure; in vain have I washed my hands in innocence (Psalm 73:13).

Asaph makes great claims for himself. He says he has been a man of moral purity and innocence and yet he suffers the result of his envy. He is plagued day and night by thoughts of what the wicked have and what he does not have. Self-pity is like that. The mind becomes engrossed in a morbid, temporal perspective. Asaph himself says that his self-pity has lead to his own ignorance and a sense of depression and oppression (v. 14,16). He also speaks of an embittered spirit and grief as a result of his self-pity. All he can see is the prosperity of the wicked and his own lack.

Many of us have experienced what Asaph has. We are so consumed by others, whom we consider evil, doing well that we can only think about them and what they have done. Instead of leaving the hurt in the past they continue to hurt us as we relive the event. Sometimes long after the initial infraction we are still bound by the memory. When we try to figure it all out we often have the same reaction as Asaph:

> When I tried to understand all this, it was oppressive to
> me... (Psalm 73:16).

Have you ever tried to understand why God lets something
happen and it seems you're not getting any answers? I can
imagine Asaph is in that situation in this psalm. Perhaps he
had been in this state for several days crying out to God;
calling out for answers and questioning God for not
responding. Many of us have been there. There seems to be
no justice. Yet it may be that the questions Asaph was asking
were not the right ones. *Perhaps Asaph was looking for a
way of fixing the situation when what he needed was a new
way of understanding it.* I have a deep conviction that often
when we think we need our circumstances to change what
we really need is a change of perspective. We need a way of
seeing our situation that gives it new meaning. That is what
Asaph found.

Asaph: perspective found

> When I tried to understand all this, it was oppressive to
> me till I entered the sanctuary of God; then I understood
> their final destiny (Psalm 73:16-17).

Asaph was overcome by trying to understand it all until he
got a new perspective. The new perspective was that of being
able to look at the situation as God did. Asaph began to see
that God is true to His word about the wicked. They will see
destruction but according to God's schedule and not ours.
The psalmist indicates that the wicked are always at the edge

of destruction (v.18). They may not know it but they are in imminent danger of God's judgment. If He seems to delay, it is for a reason, and we must be content to let Him handle things His way. When He is ready to judge them it will be swift and complete (vss. 19-20).

In verses 21-28 Asaph speaks in such wonderful language of his relationship with God that one would think it was a different writer altogether. What caused the change of perspective? Why would someone who was ready to give up on his relationship with God now be speaking of how close God is to him and how God holds his hand and leads him?

The answer lies in verse 17. He was feeling down, caught up in the perspective of one who is not trusting God until he entered God's presence and understood. This is the verse that gripped me the first time I read it. It makes so much sense that if you want to understand what is going on you spend time with the One who knows. You talk to Him, you reaffirm your love for Him, you reaffirm your commitment to Him regardless of whether or not you get the full answer. After all, He is the sovereign Lord whose understanding is far beyond ours. There will be some things we just won't understand and that shouldn't bother us because we do know that God is faithful and all powerful and He will do the right thing at the right time.

> The secret things belong to the LORD our God, but the things revealed belong to us and to our children for ever, that we may follow all the words of this law (Deut. 29:29).

God tells us what we need to know to enjoy and serve Him.

If we need to know something He will show us. If He doesn't tell us the answer to the question we are asking, then we know that either it is not for us to know or it is not time for us to know it. I know that is difficult to contemplate if you are reading this, having struggled with something that has deeply hurt you. I want to encourage you, however, that there may be a better way of thinking about your struggle. It comes from applying the principle that Asaph discovered. A principle we will develop in more detail.

Entering God's sanctuary

> Therefore, since we have a great high priest who has gone through the heavens, Jesus the Son of God, let us hold firmly to the faith we profess. For we do not have a high priest who is unable to sympathize with our weaknesses, but we have one who has been tempted in every way, just as we are – yet was without sin. Let us then approach the throne of grace with confidence, so that we may receive mercy and find grace to help us in our time of need (Heb. 4:14-16).

The Right Attitude

How do we enter the sanctuary of God? There are several concepts we need to have firmly in place as we consider approaching Him.

First, we do it with all humility. We don't approach God demanding an answer. We approach Him with the realization that had Jesus not gone to the cross on our behalf we would have no right to approach Him at all. We approach with confidence not in our cause or in ourselves but we approach with confidence in the fact that Jesus has cleared the way, through His work as mediator, for us.

Second, we approach Him in faith. We know He knows all things. We know He is a good God. In faith we must accept that whatever His answer is it is in accordance with His good and faithful character, even if our answer does not reveal why something has happened to us.

Third, we know Jesus understands. When Jesus was on earth He experienced every kind of struggle that we do. He did it without sin but that does not mean He did not experience it with intensity and struggle. He sweated blood from the intensity of the moment in the garden of Gethsemane and cried out from the cross concerning the isolation He was experiencing. He has been there. He has been a victim of physical and verbal abuse, He has been abandoned by friends and family, He has been hungry and tired, He faced both military and demonic forces, He has been murdered at the hands of people He could have destroyed with a word and all because He was more committed to who He was as an obedient Son than He was to temporal peace and comfort.

Fourth, we accept that our call from God is to obedience. Whether we understand what has happened to us or not we obey. That is really at the heart of faith, isn't it? We trust Him for those things we do not see (Heb. 11:1). If we don't understand, there is a reason. We must trust that He knows best what we need to know.

Fifth, when we approach God we accept the mercy (forgiveness and comfort) and grace (empowerment to get through the struggle) He provides. We don't need to get revenge. Vengeance belongs to the Lord. We need to gain

perspective – God's perspective. Then we can go on with
our focus on God and His calling for us. We can leave the
hurt or the person who hurt us in God's hands because that
situation or person is no longer our responsibility nor should
they be our focus.

The Right Method

There are many ways people experience the presence of God.
Following are some elements of entering His presence that
should be present as we come to Him and seek to draw near
to Him.

First, God's Word is central to all worship. Scripture is
the means by which God speaks clearly and without error.
We can trust His Word. We will not know God intimately
unless we know His Word. As the Holy Spirit works within
us to understand what we read we will be encouraged. It is
interesting to note that Asaph understood what would be
the end of the wicked people he was bothered about, but he
never did find out why they were more materially prosperous
than he was. God's Word often changes our perspective so
that we find the question we started with doesn't matter any
more.

Second, worship must also be part of the process.
Worship is for God. When we sing and lift up prayers and
praise it is to Him. Worship is the proper response for us to
make to our God. God wants us to engage in worship and
when we do we are drawn in to a rich fellowship with Him.
Worship should involve other Christians in a church setting
where the sacraments and preaching of the Word are present.
It should also be done alone through prayer and personal
devotions. Singing and praising God are activities He enjoys

and blesses. When we draw near to Him in this way He draws near to us as well.

Third, prayer and fasting are important elements to develop. Jesus engaged in prayer and fasting. Daniel too had a regular time of prayer and was tossed into the lions' den for it (Daniel was happy that the lions were fasting at the time). Fasting is something that we don't hear as much about as prayer but through fasting people can develop a sensitivity to God's leading that other disciplines don't develop so keenly. I knew of one man who fasted regularly every Monday using his lunch and dinner breaks to spend extra time in prayer and the study of Scripture. He spoke of great benefits from the practice.

Fourth, fellowship with other believers encourages our walk with God in unique ways. The writer of Hebrews made sure that people did not miss this aspect of the Christian experience (Heb. 10:25). God uses other people to encourage and teach us. If we are to understand God we must develop our relationships with His people.

Finally, I want to mention ministry. We begin to understand the things of God as we put those things into action. Responding to intimacy with God by serving others and using the gifts He has given us adds a fulness to the relationship that we would not get otherwise. Remember what was said earlier in Chapter 3? Grace is at work as we work. When we use the gifts God has given us and actively obey Him by serving others, we develop an intimacy with God akin to comaraderie. We have a sense of being on the same team and playing a significant role in the outworking of His plan.

Putting self-pity behind us

We may have good reason to be sad about what has happened
to us, but self-pity is the wrong way to respond to it. When
we engage in self-pity we are in a position of pride and
mistrust. Pride in that we say through our self-pity, 'I am
too good for this', or, 'I don't deserve this'. It is mistrust in
that we are not trusting in the providence of God. God is the
ruler of the universe and we must trust that what He allows
He allows for a good reason. We may not understand what
the reason is, but we do understand that what He wants us
to do now is trust Him and go on with life in obedience to
Him.

We put self-pity behind us in the same way we deal with
the sin of pride. We humbly affirm that what is most
important is that we trust Him, confess our own sins and
ask His help to turn from them. We then forgive those who
have wronged us and press on with what He would have us
do. As we do this we consciously leave the hurt for Him to
deal with in His own way. Every time I am tempted to
entertain the old feelings of self-pity I remind myself, and
God, that I do not own that situation any more. I have given
it to God and I must refuse to take it back. As I do that each
time I am tempted, the temptation becomes easier to handle
the next time and I gain more and more freedom from it.

Understanding self-pity helped Jean understand better why
she did some of the destructive things in her past. She used
to feel sorry for herself and tell herself she might as well
'get high' or overeat or commit adultery. After all, who
would really care. She was never good enough for her parents
anyway so she might as well act like they expected her to

act. While Jean was glad that those days were behind her, she realized that as a Christian she could still be tempted to ungodly living if she did not remain on her guard and continue to draw near to God. If she had learned anything since becoming a Christian it was that temptation doesn't vanish for the Christian, it just puts on more clever disguises. But Jean also learned another perspective that continues to help. She learned that God calls all of His children to make a pilgrimage through this life and into the eternal presence of God. She learned that it was not her place to be concerned whether someone else had a 'better' pilgrimage than she did. Jean found that her pilgrimage is unique and the task for her is to accept what happens as her journey is designed to make her more like her Savior. So whether the road is rough or smooth Jean works at being content and faithful to follow God wherever He leads.

It is because Jesus has broken the stranglehold of sin that we no longer have to be so preoccupied with self. May God grant all of us the grace and mercy to be people who are not engaged in the ungodly exhibition which is self-pity.

Section 4

The Purpose

The great overarching goal of the Christian life is obedience to the King. And he is pleased when we obey.[29] *(R.C. Sproul)*

Question. 1. What is the chief and highest end of man?
Answer: Man's chief and highest end is to glorify God, and fully to enjoy Him for ever. *(The Larger Catechism of the Westminster Confession of Faith, 1648)*

Could it be you make your presence known
So often by your absence?
Could it be that questions tell us more
Than answers ever do?
Could it be that you would really
Rather die than live without us?
Could it be the only answer
That means anything is you?[30]

Michael Card

Chapter 11

Loving God With All That You Are

In these final pages I am going to explain how we can overcome our past and apply the truth of the Scriptures in a way that brings about change which is lasting and change which makes us more like Christ. But why? Why go to all the trouble of changing habits and thought patterns? Can't we just believe in Jesus and muddle through life as we always have? No. Not if we want to find God's best. Not if we want to fulfil our calling. You see, there really is a better way to live. It is to discover a purpose for our lives that transcends everything else; a purpose that makes all the struggle worth it. Wouldn't it be wonderful to live for something worth dying for?

What is your reason for living? Do you have an organizing principle in your life that governs your thoughts, feelings and decisions? A friend once told me her life just wasn't working out as she had planned. She explained that after she became a Christian she felt much excitement and renewal in her life, but now a year later it didn't seem real any more. I knew about her past and the guilt she had struggled with. I knew how coming to Christ had made her feel forgiven and renewed. Now, however, the smile was hard to find and she was about to give up. I asked, 'Did you become a Christian because of how it made you feel or did you become a Christian because Christianity is true?' She looked at me like she thought I had asked her a trick question. When she saw I was serious she hesitatingly said, 'I guess it was because of how it made me feel.' I quickly explained that feelings were never designed to carry us through the Christian life. We need something larger and stronger than our feelings to carry us through the struggles that inevitably come. We need what some refer to as an organizing principle, a goal or purpose for life that is more important than our feelings, indeed one which is more important than we are.

People today have become so self-involved that they have bought in to the notion that personal happiness and fulfilment are the most important qualities of life. Even Christians have accepted these ideals. But that is not the way it was supposed to be. 'In the beginning God created...' (Gen. 1:1). God was in the beginning as Creator. As Creator He designed the purpose for His creation. If we are going to be the people we were created to be, we must live according to the Creator's design. Our purpose in life must be whatever He says it should be.

What is that goal we are always to keep in clear focus? The Bible says it in several different ways. The way I find the most encompassing and easiest to understand was spoken of by the Lord Himself.

One of the teachers of the law came and heard them debating. Noticing that Jesus had given them a good answer, he asked him, 'Of all the commandments, which is the most important?'

'The most important one,' answered Jesus, 'is this: "Hear, O Israel, the Lord our God, the Lord is one. Love the Lord your God with all your heart and with all your soul and with all your mind and with all your strength."

The second is this: "Love your neighbor as yourself."
There is no commandment greater than these' (Mark
12:28-31).

A man illustrated this as he explained his desperate
situation to me. 'I know God hates divorce, but doesn't He
also want me to be happy?' I didn't respond, so he went on,
'I just don't love her anymore, maybe I never did. We were
so young. So I just don't see how staying married could be
what God wants since I'm so unhappy.'

I finally responded, 'You seem to place the emphasis on
being happy. Is that what you see as the goal of your life?'

'Well, I don't know if it's the goal,' he said hesitatingly,
'but doesn't God want me to be happy?'

Our initial reaction may be 'Yes'. Closer scrutiny,
however, reveals that the question itself is self-oriented. Its
concern is for the person asking it. What if we change the
question to read, 'How can I make God happy?' Now the
question is God-oriented and places self in the position of
servant. To put it simply, if you want to have the break with
your past that really means something for all eternity, a break
with the tragedy and struggle you have known, you must
stop asking, 'How can I be happy?' and begin asking, 'How
can I make God happy?' It is not that our enjoyment of life
is unimportant, it is just that it is a by-product of serving
God, not the goal of life.

It all begins with love
Making God happy may seem like a wonderful idea but it
can also seem very difficult. Part of the reason may be that
we think of love as something we feel. But is it? I remember

being a bit perplexed the first time someone told me that
love was more of a decision than a warm feeling. After I
thought about it, however, it made sense. Jesus had said we
should love our enemies (Matt.5:44). I can't think of any
enemies for whom I have warm, positive feelings and yet I
am supposed to love them. This has implications for our
love for God. There are times when we are torn in our
loyalties to Him and are tempted to give in to the love of
self over and above our love of God. If, however, we make
the decision to love God regardless of how we feel, we begin
to have victory over temptation. It begins with a decision
and comes to fruition as we act in accordance with that
decision and do the thing that pleases Him. Love of God
involves obedience to Him. As Jesus said: 'If you love me,
you will obey what I command' (John 14:15).

Loving God His way

The love of God involves nothing less than the whole person.
We love Him by first making the decision to do so and then
by devoting all that we are to the task of loving Him. Dying
to self and loving God do not mean that we avoid pleasant
experiences, nor do they mean doing only those things that
we want to do. They do mean that we must not participate
in sin and that what we do we do with the express purpose
of bringing honor to the Lord. At times we will suffer, at
times we will experience pleasure, but neither suffering nor
pleasure is the goal. The goal is to love God across the whole
spectrum of our lives.

Putting it into practice

Jesus not only told us that we are to love God, He also told us *how* we are to love God. He broke it down for us to emphasize that the totality of our being is involved in loving Him. Let's examine the different aspects of who we are as Jesus presented them – heart, soul, strength and mind.

Loving God with your heart

Loving God with all your heart may not sound strange at all. We often speak of loving someone with all our heart. Biblically, however, the heart is not simply the seat of the affections. Dick Keyes defines the heart as, 'The inmost core of the self, your psychological and spiritual center of gravity.'[31] In responding to the words of Jesus, 'For where your treasure is, there will your heart be also' (Matt. 6:21), Keyes points out that the heart resides where the treasure is. How wonderful it is to place our treasure in doing the will of God. As the prophet said, 'The one who trusts [in Messiah] will never be dismayed' (Isa. 28:16). Loving God with our hearts is something lasting. We can never get enough nor will we ever be disappointed by Him. In the deepest recesses of who I am I am safe and secure because my treasure is found not in the fleeting treasure of this world but in the love of God.

Loving God with your soul

Most often we think of the soul as the immaterial part of man in its broadest application. In the present context the soul is the seat of man's emotional activity.[32] This means that when we love God with our souls we are loving Him emotionally. In our day of seeking to do what feels right this is an especially important concept to understand. In our relationship with God, as in any relationship, we must train our emotions to be loyal. A husband or a wife must not allow romantic emotions for another to develop. Emotions don't 'just happen', they are allowed to grow. In relation to God we must train our emotions to love only Him, allowing no other gods a place in our souls.

As we spend time in worship, prayer, the study of His Word, and in ministry to others out of love for Him, we will see our emotional lives conform more and more to the image of Christ and we will spend less time absorbed with self.

Loving God with your mind

In our culture the intellectual has been played down in favor of 'just believing', or it has been replaced with snappy slogans and superficial approaches to theology and worship. If we are to love God with our minds we must affirm the import-ance of thinking as a Christian and the hard work it takes to develop our minds.[33] That is why the apostle Paul puts such stress on mind renewal in Romans 12:2:

> Do not conform any longer to the pattern of this world, but be transformed by the renewing of your mind. Then you will be able to test and approve what God's will is – his good, pleasing and perfect will.

According to the apostle, if we are going to avoid conformity to the world and if we are going to know the will of God, it will be through the renewal of the mind. The mind is the place where ideas start. If we think biblically our ideas will be God-honoring. But the mind also is the place of basic attitudes and dispositions.[34] If the mind is renewed according to Scripture, our attitudes will be pleasing to God and not so susceptible to self-centred reactions. Our relationships will improve as we are not so caught up in self and are able to discern situations maturely, accurately, and with compassion.

How is the mind renewed? Let me give you four principles to get you started.

1. Get to know God in a richer, deeper way. Begin spending much more time in Bible study and reading Christian literature which takes you deeper in your understanding of God and the Christian life.[35]

2. Pray. We must converse with God about the things we are experiencing and the things we are studying. We must ask God to help us think as a Christian and change the old patterns in favor of the truth. We must not underestimate the importance of this great privilege of prayer.

3. You must begin speaking the truth to yourself. When thoughts come to mind telling you how inadequate you are, you must begin telling yourself the truth concerning your true identity in Christ. It is more important to know what God says about the situation than to believe some warmed-over lie from the past. But you must also begin to behave in accordance with the truth. Right thinking must be accompanied by right behavior to please God.

4. Get a friend or a fellowship group together of mature, growing Christians who will be accountable to you and you to them. Learn to speak the truth in love to one another when you talk about your problems or joys in unbiblical ways. If you are prone to self-pity you need someone to point out to you the times you slip into the 'Why me?' syndrome.

Loving God with your strength

Strength, in Mark 12:30, refers to power or might.[36] By including it here the Lord brings into focus the fact that all of our energy is to be put into loving Him. If we are inclined to think we are doing pretty well in our devotion to God, this passage reminds us that our love for Him must be full devotion. But there is a danger here. The danger is what J.I. Packer refers to as 'the religion of busyness'. We must not mistake being busy with being spiritual. We must pick our priorities before the Lord. Doing more is not necessarily more pleasing to God. We must fulfil our calling as it is spelled out in Scripture. When it is time to work, we work with all our strength. When it is time to rest, we rest with all our strength. There is a time to work and a time to rest and we should do both for the love of God.

Tying them all together

When Jesus said we are to love God with all these aspects of our being, it was another way of saying that every part of man is involved in loving God. If one part is not pursuing the love of God, the whole is affected as well.

Think of the ingredients of a cake. I am not a chef but I know that there are many ingredients that go into baking a cake. I also know that you get all these ingredients together and mix them up before you begin baking. If you tried to cook the parts separately I don't know what you would get, but it would not be a cake. Yet when it is properly prepared, with all of the ingredients mixed together, it's quite good. Like-wise, we must not attempt to live 'part' of our lives before God and the other 'parts' in some other way. That sort of life is not a life of love for Him and it is extremely distasteful to our Creator.[37]

Loving your neighbor

God does not tell us to love Him only. He also tells us to love others. Love of our neighbor flows from a heart that loves God. If we were left with only the first great commandment, loving God, perhaps someone could make a case for retreating to a place of serenity and communing with God. That, however, is not what God has in mind. By Jesus including the second command with the first, He is assuring that our love of God is not self-centred. He makes certain that we do not retreat but that we become involved in expressing the love of God to those around us. His command forces us to be involved in human relationships.

This is extremely important in an age that is so self-oriented. Jesus went to the cross because of His love for God the Father and His love for human beings in need of salvation. We too are to love God and love others, with our lives if necessary.

... as yourself

When Jesus says to love others as we love ourselves He is not commanding us to love self. The command is to love others. Love of self in recent years has been treated as a goal, when actually it has been part of the human makeup all along. God instilled in man at his creation a *healthy* love for self. If it were not so, the command would not make sense.

If I am hungry I find food, or try to. If I am sick I try to get well or at least to lessen the pain. Jesus tells us that just as we love ourselves and would do whatever we could to care for our needs, so should we be committed to the needs of others.

Love of God was never meant to stand alone. We are to love others every bit as much as we love ourselves. Just imagine what the world would be like if Christians really did this.

Why is love the greatest?
At the end of the great chapter on love in 1 Corinthians 13 the apostle says this:

> And now these three remain: faith, hope and love. But the greatest of these is love (1 Cor. 13:13).

Why is it that love is the greatest of these three virtues? William Hendriksen offers three reasons:[38]

1. Faith and hope take, love gives. Faith appropriates the salvation that is in Christ. Hope accepts the promise of the future inheritance. Love, however, means self-giving, self-impartation.

2. All other virtues are included in love. According to 1 Corinthians 13 active, intelligent, voluntary love implies patience, kindness and humility (verse 4), unselfishness (verse 5), faith and hope (verse 7).

3. Human love, in its noblest expression, is patterned after God, for 'God is love'. Love gives, but the reason we are able to give it is because God loved us first (1 John 4:19). Only as we love God and love others in increasing measure will we be able to engage successfully in the process of growth in the Christian life. Then we can leave the past behind and experience the life He desires for us.

It is my prayer that as you seek to apply the things written in these pages you would do so for the love of God and for the furtherance of His kingdom. In so doing you will experience what it is to live as a child of the King. You will discover the abundant life Jesus spoke of:

I came that they might have life, and might have it abundantly (John 10:10b).

Epilogue:

A Victim No More

'I have some news for you.' Jean's voice was clear and excited. I hadn't heard from her in a while so I had no idea what she might be thinking of.

'What is it?' I asked.

'I'm pregnant.'

'That's wonderful,' I replied. 'How do you feel about that?'

Although Jean's voice had sounded excited I knew that as recently as a year before she was not at all certain about having children. She had always wanted them but wasn't sure she could handle them. But she explained how her attitude was different now. She now looked on the future with hope concerning what God would do in her life and the life of her family. Where once she feared she would turn out like her parents and would not wish to bring up a child as they had, she now knew that, in Christ, she was breaking the cycle of the past and could help her child do the same.

Perhaps the greatest change Jean discovered was that she no longer feared the future. That was because she now understood that the role of victim was no longer her part to play. Christ had set her free from all that. For so much of her life she had believed she was doomed to repeat the cycle. Pop-psychology had only confirmed this. But no more would she be the victim. In Christ she had the power to look problems straight in the face and refuse to give in to self-pity. Now every time the old tapes played the abuse of her parents in her mind, she could resist them as lies from hell and reaffirm that as a child of the King she no longer had to listen to such rubbish. If there was a problem, she faced it with the truth of God's Word. If she sinned she didn't look for others to blame, she confessed her sin, repented and pressed on, determined to love Him more. She knew she was not perfect, but she knew she was on the right road and that on this road there were no victims – just washed sinners who had been granted the highest privilege of all – the privilege of becoming children of God and growing up to be like their Father.

May His people travel that road with all diligence as the days are evil and His return imminent.

Notes

[1] As quoted by Michael Scott Horton in *Putting Amazing Back Into Grace*, p.223. Published by Thomas Nelson.

[2] John White, *Parents in Pain*, Inter Varsity Press, Downers Grove, IL, p. 53.

[3] We will discuss the application of His provision for guilt and shame further in Chapter 3.

[4] When man fell he experienced brokenness in at least four areas. His separation from God, himself, others and nature. For a more complete study of this see *Genesis in Space and Time* by Francis A. Schaeffer, Tyndale House Publishers, 1972.

[5] From John Owen, *The Works of John Owen*, Vol. VI, Banner of Truth Trust, p. 7.

[6] Ferguson, Sinclair B.; Wright, David F.; Packer, J.I.; Editors *New Dictionary of Theology*, InterVarsity Press, Downers Grove, IL 1988.

[7] See *Doubt* by Os Guinness, InterVarsity Press, 1976. This is an excellent work on the nature of our spiritual experience as we struggle to live by faith.

[8] 'The Curse of Self-Esteem', *Newsweek*, February 17, 1992, pp. 46-51.

[9] Ranald Macaulay and Jerram Barrs, *Being Human: The Nature of Spiritual Experience*, InterVarsity Press, 1978, pp. 13-14.

[10] Dick Keyes, *Beyond Identity*, Servant Books, 1984, p. 36.

[11] *Ibid.*, p. 38.

[12] Concerning how a Christian should think about himself or herself, Sinclair B. Ferguson says: 'Our self-image, if it is to be biblical, will begin just here. God is my Father (the Christian's self-image always begins with the knowledge of God and who He is); I am one of His children (I know my real identity); His people are my brothers and sisters (I recognize the family to which I belong, and have discovered my deepest "roots")', Sinclair B. Ferguson, *Children of the Living God*, Navpress, 1987, p. 18.

[13] For a great study on prayer in its many forms see *Pray With Your Eyes Open* by Richard Pratt, Presbyterian and Reformed Publishing, 1986.

[14] See *True Spirituality* by Francis A. Schaeffer, InterVarsity Press, 1975, for a more complete study of the nature of spiritual experience this side of heaven.

[15] See *No God But God* Eds. Guinness and Seel, Chapter 4, 'More Victimized Than Thou' for an excellent discussion on the Christian and victimization.

[16] Francis A. Schaeffer, *True Spirituality*, InterVarsity Press, 1975, p. 133.

[17] For a study of Dr. Van Til's teaching on this see *Every Thought Captive* by Richard Pratt, Presbyterian and Reformed Publishing, 1983. For an introduction to the apologetics of Van Til see K. Scott Oliphint, *Cornelius Van Til and the Reformation of Christian Apologetics* (Order from: Westminster Discount Book Service, Inc. P.O. Box 125H Scarsdale, New York 10583).

[18] See also Matthew 5:1-12; 1 Corinthians 6:9-10; Ephesians 5:5; and Revelation 22:15.

[19]There will be more discussion of the Christian mind in the last chapter of this book.

[20] I am especially indebted to the work of Dr. Jay Adams in regards to the application of Ephesians 4:22-24 to personal change. See *Helping People Change*, Presbyterian and Reformed Publishing Company, Phillipsburg, New Jersey 1973.

[21]For a helpful study on speaking the truth of Scripture to yourself see: Backus, William and Chapian, *Marie Telling Yourself the Truth*, Bethany House Publishers, 1980.

[22]For a discussion of the dynamic role of the church in the life of the Christian see *The Body* by Chuck Colson, Word Publishing, Dallas, London, Vancouver, Melbourne, 1992.

[23]See *The Gravedigger File* by Os Guinness, InterVarsity Press, Downers Grove, IL, 1983.

[24] See *The Blessing* by Gary Smalley and John Trent, Thomas Nelson, Inc., Nashville, TN, 1986, for a discussion of five key elements children need from their parents for personal stability.

[25] Dick Keyes, *Beyond Identity*, Servant Books, Ann Arbor, Michigan, 1984, p. 172.

[26]*Ibid.*, pp. 180-1.

[27]For a good discussion of the subject of repressed memories see: Ed Bulkley, *Only God Can Heal the Wounded Heart*, Harvest House Publishers, 1995.

[28] Dick Keyes, *Beyond Identity*, p. 145.

[29]From *Pleasing God* by R.C. Sproul, Tyndale, 1988, p.32.

[30]From 'Could it Be' by Michael Card from the Album *Present Reality*, The Sparrow Corporation, 1988.

[31]Dick Keyes, *Beyond Identity*, Servant Books, Ann Arbor, Michigan, p. 13.

[32]William Hendriksen, *The Gospel of Mark*, New Testament Commentary Series, Baker Book House, Grand Rapids, Michigan, 1975, p. 493.

[33]See Os Guinness, *Fit Bodies Fat Minds: Why Evangelicals Don't Think and What to Do About It*, Hourglass Books/Baker Books, 1994.

[34]*Ibid*. p. 493

[35]Contemporary books such as *Knowing God* by J.I. Packer, *Know Your Christian Life* by Sinclair Ferguson or *The Holiness of God* by R.C. Sproul will all help to expand your perception of the God we worship. Remember too the classics such as *Pilgrim's Progress* by John Bunyan, *Holiness* by J.C. Ryle (Evangelical Press), *Way of Holiness* by Ken Prior (Christian Focus Publiations, 1995) or *The Practice of Godliness* by Abraham Kuyper as well as biographies of heroes of the faith.

[36]William Hendriksen, *The Gospel of Mark*, p. 493.

[37] See John 14:15 and Mark 12:30. Study also what Jesus says to the Pharisees in Matthew 23. The Pharisees were guilty of acting in a righteous way but having cold, selfish hearts toward God. Jesus lets them know that both the heart and behavior must reflect God's righteousness.

[38]William Hendriksen, *The Gospel of Mark*, p. 494-495.

SCRIPTURE INDEX

INDEX

Those Ugly Emotions

How to manage negative emotions

Ken M. Campbell

This book is a guide to managing negative feelings and using them constructively to develop a closer relationship with the Lord. While psychologically sound, it is not a psychology book; rather, it stresses the role of the Word of God in living our lives.

Ken M Campbell is an Associate Professor of Biblical Studies at Belhaven College in Jackson, Mississippi. A native of Scotland, he has pastored churches in the U.K. and the U.S.A. He is married and has one daughter. He holds degrees from the University of Aberdeen, Scotland (MA), Westminster Theological Seminary, Philadelphia (BD, ThM), and the University of Manchester, England (PhD).

'It is a pleasure to commend this book by Dr. Campbell entitled *Those Ugly Emotions*. It is a book in which he endeavours to help the reader manage what he calls 'negative emotions'. Ken guides us in the way in which God expects us to deal with seven emotions: fear, depression, anger, guilt, hatred, envy and jealousy, and grief. The book is filled with anecdotal material which helps illustrate the points that are made. Perhaps the greatest benefit is in the way in which one learns to *use* the Psalms in meeting many experiences in life.'

Jay Adams

ISBN 1 85792 244 1

Bill Hines (B.A. Political Science; M.A. Counseling; M.A. Religion) is the President of Covenant Ministries, Inc., a biblical counselling and education ministry in Ft. Worth, Texas. Bill has undertaken graduate studies at Liberty University, Reformed Theological Seminary and the Francis A. Schaeffer Institute at Covenant Theological Seminary. In addition to his work as a counselor Bill writes a monthly column in the *Dallas/Ft. Worth Heritage* newspaper and for the monthly newsletter *Pressing On*, a publication of Covenant Ministries, Inc. He serves as adjunct faculty for LeTourneau University and Trinity Bible College and Seminary.

An ordained minister since 1985 Bill is licensed to preach the Gospel with the North Texas Presbytery of the Presbyterian Church in America and is a member of the National Association of Nouthetic Counselors and the International Association of Biblical Counselors.

He and his wife, Kathy, have four daughters and one son.

Address Correspondence and Seminar Inquiries to :

Covenant Ministries, Inc.

P.O. Box 121235

Ft. Worth, TX 76121-1235 U.S.A.